Making Middle Schools Work

Jon Wiles and
Joseph Bondi

Association for Supervision
and Curriculum Development

125 N. West Street
Alexandria, VA 22314-2798
703/549-9110

Copyright 1986 by the
Association for Supervision and Curriculum Development
125 N. West Street
Alexandria, VA 22314-1798

All rights reserved. No part of this publication may be reproduced or transmitted in any form or by any means, electronic or mechanical, including photocopy, recording, or any information storage and retrieval system, without permission in writing from the publisher.

ASCD publications present a variety of viewpoints. The views expressed or implied in this publication are not necessarily official positions of the Association.

Price $7.25

ASCD Stock Number: 611-86046
ISBN: 0-87120-139-9
Library of Congress Catalog Card Number: 86-71816

Making Middle Schools Work

Foreword	vii
Introduction	1
1. The Changing Roles of Intermediate Education	3
2. Setting the Stage for Meaningful Change	12
3. Designing Middle School Programs for Success	20
4. People Make Middle Schools Work	31
5. The Promises Must Be Kept	38
References	58
Appendix A. Sample Survey Instruments and Forms	59
Appendix B. Characteristics of Emerging Adolescents: Implications for the Middle School	84
Appendix C. Selected Teacher Competencies for Middle School Teachers	88
Appendix D. Emerging Adolescents: Victims of a Changing Society	91

About the Authors

Jon Wiles and Joseph Bondi have worked together as authors and consultants since 1977. They have co-authored six major texts on curriculum, supervision, and school administration as well as numerous articles and professional papers. Their book, *The Essential Middle School* (1980), ranks as the best-selling book on the topic. Their consulting firm, Wiles, Bondi, and Associates, has worked with educational agencies and schools in forty states and ten foreign nations. During the past five years they have specialized in curriculum development in large-city districts such as Denver, St. Louis, Baton Rouge, Orlando, and Dallas. Wiles, Bondi, and Associates is located at 213 Park Ridge, Tampa, FL 33617.

Foreword

BASED ON THEIR BELIEF THAT TRUE MIDDLE SCHOOLS MUST BE ROOTED in terms of human growth and development, Jon Wiles and Joseph Bondi provide a practical book to advance this distinctly American educational concept. Drawn primarily from their experience as consultants in a variety of school districts, *Making Middle Schools Work* offers a wealth of resources for those seeking to establish or improve middle schools.

It is an appropriate and important sequel to their popular 1980 publication, *The Essential Middle School*.

Their approach is to superimpose a management plan on a curriculum development framework. It is this Curriculum Management Plan generated by the authors that provides the focus for this book.

From a discussion of the changing roles of intermediate education, the authors explain the need for accurate data on which to base meaningful change, describe the designing of successful programs, examine the specific aspects of staff development, and emphasize the significance of mechanisms for feedback and evaluation to inform, impress, and sustain progress.

The central thread throughout the entire document is the provision of a comprehensive and balanced curriculum focused on the development of individuals rather than attainment of knowledge. This thread provides meaning to the many documents assembled from different sources as examples of key elements in the Curriculum Management Plan.

A basic premise is that the elaborate and comprehensive committee structure of the plan creates an advocacy group that compensates for changes among board members, superintendents, other leadership personnel, and teachers committed to the middle school. In this manner, progress can be maintained toward goal attainment, despite replacements at all levels that have caused districts to postpone, modify, or abandon the middle school concept.

While it is unlikely that this book would itself recruit school leaders or teachers to the middle school movement, encouragement in this direction is highly likely. More significantly, for those engaged in the difficult task of curriculum development as the entry point to creating middle schools, the authors share insights, information, and inspiration that should prove extremely valuable.

GERALD R. FIRTH
ASCD President, 1986-87

Introduction

THE MIDDLE SCHOOL IN AMERICA IS TWO DECADES OLD. HOW QUICKLY those years have passed since the term "middle school" was coined by William Alexander in the mid-1960s. For 20 years this educational phenomenon has been unfolding in practice environments, and it is highly appropriate for the Association for Supervision and Curriculum Development to assess its status. Has the middle school been a success? Can the concept really be made to work?

In the early years, the term middle school was given to those junior high schools that deviated from a standardized intermediate program. Usually these innovative junior highs had exciting principals who stacked the regular program with special innovations like team teaching or a modular-flexible schedule. Most of the early literature addressed these special schools and their specific innovations.

Those early writings must have struck a nerve among intermediate educators, because a grassroots following soon emerged through state organizations and such national organizations as ASCD and the National Middle School Association. The number of middle schools grew quickly as monitored by survey after survey in the late 1960s and early 1970s. During this time, a definition emerged of a new intermediate school, organized around a period of human development.

Stimulating this growth, of course, were many noneducational variables like a slight over-enrollment and desegregation. In reality, these factors had greater effect on the spread of middle schools than did educational logic. They provided an opportunity for development and experimentation, and more and more schools took on the characteristics of the "reformed" junior high.

By the mid-1970s the pervasive logic of the true middle school, a school especially designed for the preadolescent learner, began to take hold. The middle school concept was reinforced by a growing body of research suggesting the true uniqueness of the preadolescent: neither child nor adolescent, but rather someone in transition between these two more stable conditions.

Finally, in the late 1970s, the real middle school came into focus, complete with its own textbooks, a large national following, and self-help organizations in most states. The American middle school had arrived, replacing 80 percent of the nation's 9,500 junior high schools in the short space of two decades. It was a phenomenon indeed!

But there was an Achilles heel to this education success story. Throughout the United States, many schools were slipping back into the old form. Even the so-called model middle schools that had received so much attention were becoming less innovative and more standardized. It was reported that teachers in the middle school "burned out"; that turnover among principals, superintendents, and board members resulted in lost commitment. Critics said the middle school concept could not be sustained.

We certainly observed this slippage on a regular basis. It was not unusual to consult with a district on middle school development in the 1960s only to return 10 or 15 years later in order to completely reinvent the concept. Identifying model schools was always a problem for fear that they had evaporated since the last visit. Too often, the middle school seemed to depend on an administrative personality or the benevolence of a teacher union or board. The middle school concept could only be developed and sustained under certain conditions.

We acknowledge these realities. What this book attempts to do is cut through the rhetoric and identify what it takes to make a middle school work. The prescription is based on experience, lots of it, and it requires both discipline and resources. The process also achieves dramatic results.

So that other ASCD members can benefit from our experience, *Making Middle Schools Work* contains many instruments and techniques that have proven effective in real practice environments throughout the United States. These techniques and instruments become more refined with continued use. Special recognition is due the Orange County School District of Florida, which is the source of many of our citations. The commitment of this district to developing the best possible program for preadolescents has been inspirational to us. We hope that the reader can adapt these ideas to local conditions. This truly American educational design needs all of our best efforts to make it work.

JON WILES
JOSEPH BONDI

1
The Changing Roles of Intermediate Education

FOR READERS TO FULLY COMPREHEND THE APPROACH WE PRESCRIBE here, it is necessary to review how the middle school design seeks to change the way a school functions and the rationale for that change.

In the period between 1910-1915, the junior high school emerged in America in response to certain needs and problems. The experiment with a six-year high school (the 6-6 plan) had proved a failure characterized by attrition and morale problems. New and exciting literature on human development, based on studies like those of Edward Hall, prompted an innovative school form covering grades 7-9 and designed for early adolescents. Pressure from waves of immigrants called for a broader and thinner curriculum. While paying lip service to the new learners, the junior high school modeled itself after the high school and used subject content as its common denominator for planning experiences.

Efforts to develop a program for new learners between the elementary and high school grades quickly failed. If understanding of the preadolescent existed, and the literature suggests it did, logistics soon overcame the best intentions to create a special school. The fact that between 1890 and 1924 the American secondary school population increased from 200,000 to almost five million students says it all.

Whatever seeds of humanism and understanding might have called forth the junior high school were soon overshadowed by more immediate concerns for buildings, teachers, and books. In short, the concept of a junior high school was lost and remained in the background of the more historic form of the American high school until the mid-1950s. Since then, the term "junior high school" has been without real meaning.

While the junior high school was launched in hard times, the American middle school was born in the best of times—an era of plentiful resources, a slight over-enrollment, fuzziness of educational philosophy, and a definite reaction to the somewhat overbearing rigidity of the post-Sputnik curriculum. The early 1960s saw the emergence of education as a science. Anything seemed possible, and the best possible program was a widely shared goal.

Not surprisingly, the very best theorists of the late junior high period (Alexander, Lounsbury, Vars) emerged to pick up the thread and provide leadership for the middle school. Resurrecting the early junior high school literature, which focused on the learner, not content, these leaders projected a total program of education serving a very special learner. Like the parallel group advocating early childhood education, the middle school advocates formulated their visions in terms of human growth and development rather than a ladder of content in subject areas. This critical distinction has remained submerged for 20 years and is the singular reason why the middle school concept retains a degree of conceptual fuzziness despite thousands of words and hundreds of speeches about the topic.[1]

Espousing a child-centered, holistic philosophy and supported by an emerging research foundation (the Berkeley Growth Studies), the early authors proposed that this new school should focus on a developmental stage characterized by the passage through puberty. Research indicated that 95 percent of all humans experience this dramatic change between ages 10-14. The program would bridge the child-centered elementary school experience and the content-directed curriculums of the high school. The program would be broad, addressing the physical, social, emotional, and intellectual needs of these preadolescents. There should be a balance among the program's various facets, said the theorists, and it should be success-oriented rather than a win-lose experience.

---

[1] The early theorists of the middle school consciously adopted the strategy of getting numbers first and worrying about the adoption of the philosophy later. In retrospect, we believe this delayed the development of real middle schools by ten years.

The meaning of these prescriptions was quickly obscured by the hype surrounding early middle school models. Reports of efforts by junior high schools to break away from standardization were given great attention, and in a short period middle school became a synonym for an innovative junior high school. Focus on the innovations rather than philosophy meant that many schools believed they had arrived when they implemented team teaching or an exploratory wheel. By 1970 the middle school movement was in trouble because it lacked definition; any grade arrangement with a few instructional wrinkles would qualify.

By and large, the promise of the middle school far outstripped its performance, and for about five years there was true concern over the concept. Repeated calls for evaluation were often met by an embarrassed silence; how can you measure what you can't define? Most practicing educators were unable to grasp the essence of a comprehensive or balanced program and failed to translate these notions into an educational design.

The changes being advocated were indeed momentous:

- programs focusing on individual student development rather than a mastery of content in subject areas.
- comprehensive curriculum addressing all important aspects of growth.
- balance (parity) between the social, emotional, physical, and intellectual dimensions of the curriculum.
- acknowledgment of the futility of education beyond elementary school for many children while promising some success for everyone.

By the early 1970s the theory-practice gap in middle school education had widened to dangerous proportions. In response to the philosophical implications of the theory, most practitioners spoke of isolated innovations, token compromises, and managerial acts such as changing a grade configuration or adopting a new schedule. This mismatch of intentions and actions imperiled implementation of the middle school. The idea seemed to rise and fall with such noneducational concerns as the economy and the return to a conservative national leadership. In some areas, the accountability movement all but killed the middle school dream.

Under these conditions and limitations the authors and many other educators labored to implement the most original and exciting educational program ever designed in the United States. Over time came the realization that there would be no shortcut to the middle school. Its philosophy was everything; it rationalized effort and provided direction on a daily basis.

What was needed was a method of getting a school or district to really understand what they were undertaking with the middle school and a managerial technique to translate that philosophy into practice. This process is the subject of *Making Middle Schools Work*.

Managing Curriculum Development in Middle Schools

At the very heart of implementing true middle schools is some good old-fashioned curriculum development. The Wiles-Bondi Curriculum Management Plan (CMP) draws from the previous work of Tyler and Taba and from the widely used accreditation process format. Put simply, the CMP attempts to introduce regularity into the process of change. Without such a logic, the pitfalls for a complex design like the middle school are multiple.

This model for curriculum development differs, for example, from an accreditation design by superimposing a management schemata over the curiculum development framework. In recognition of the political variables of local school environments, the CMP forces values clarification and commitment at each step.

A first step in any curriculum development, for instance, is to determine direction through an analysis of purpose. Our first step is to develop a working definition of the middle school to be endorsed by key decision makers (board, superintendent), thus setting up an administrative mandate. Based on this attempt at a philosophy, a deductive (if-then) logic is set in motion and proceeds all the way to what the teacher is doing in the classroom. *If* that is what we mean by "middle school," *then* where do we stand now (enter needs assessment)? *If* that is reality (needs assessment results), then what is the difference between where we are and where we want to be? *If* those are the differences, *then* which of these things (emerging goals) are most important (priorities)?

Our model is based on several key points:

1. To bring about lasting change, the people to be affected (teachers, parents, administrators, pupils) must be involved in assessing the proposed changes.

2. Change cannot happen spontaneously in a bureaucratic environment like a school district and thus must be directed from the top.

3. Decisions are best made on the basis of hard data, and such information should be open to all involved in planning.

4. Evaluation and accountability can "drive" change in schools.

The planning of a middle school thus goes through a standard curriculum development cycle of analysis, design, implementation, and evaluation. On top of this historic process CMP establishes a routine that pushes the process along and keeps it from becoming sidetracked. The entire effort can be conceptualized as a distance-rate-time problem, for as soon as we know where we are going, the resources needed to implement the plan will determine the amount of time needed to accomplish the desired ends. Because of the philosophical thrusts of the middle school design, some three to five years are required in most districts to make a complete conversion from the junior high school design. Figure 1, at page 11, provides a sample statement of philosophy.*

Management of the CMP depends heavily on committees to clarify values and provide planning direction. While committees have a negative connotation to most teachers and administrators, they are essential to the "valuing" process. To lessen resistance, the CMP uses ad hoc committees where possible, thereby making their work highly directional and product oriented. The skeletal outline of such a committee management plan looks like this:

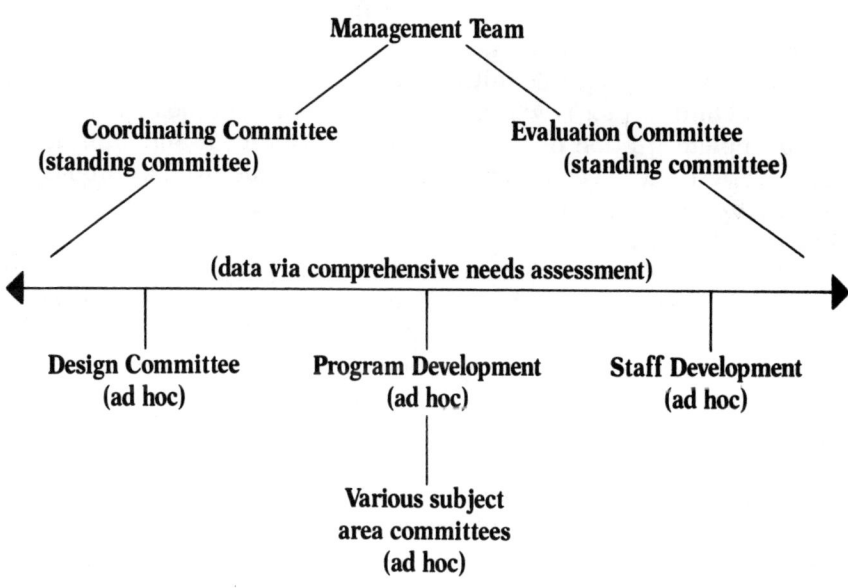

---

*All figures in this book appear at the conclusion of the chapter in which they are cited.

Essentially, a management team is composed of those district administrators who make final instructional decisions and provide resources to principals and curriculum consultants. This group initiates planning, conducts a major needs assessment, and reviews committee recommendations prior to submission to the board for approval.

The management team forms two standing committees to carry the process of curriculum change throughout the life of the project: a broadly based coordinating committee and a highly representative evaluation committee. These two groups will meet periodically to chart the course for change and to assess its progress.

Three ad hoc (nonpermanent) committees will meet to design the middle school, translate that design into prescriptions for instruction, and provide teachers with whatever skills and training are necessary to deliver the program. The design, program development, and staff development committees meet in a sequential fashion and, upon doing their work, dissolve. Such a sequencing of these tasks keeps the model pure by closely defining the task of each subsequent ad hoc group.

Moving this process along, from planning to implementation, are periodic reports to the school board that project actions and summarize accomplishments. Thus the board is sequentially asked to accept a philosophy and definition, adopt target goals and standards, accept definitions for new programs, and set aside funds for the long-term implementation of both program development and staff development activities. The reports to the board come from an impartial and representative evaluation committee, which keeps score of the ongoing change effort.

While the reader may think that this management system seems unnecessarily cumbersome, it should be remembered that slippage is the great enemy of the middle school concept. Teachers turn over, boards change, superintendents come and go; it is a rare district in the United States that can look ahead five years and carry out a plan to improve instruction. This process guarantees that the critical curriculum work will proceed uninterrupted over the long haul.

The bottom line on the CMP is that it works. The process minimizes political activity. It guarantees continuity of effort across the district. It manages change and resource allocation for the board. It eliminates single-issue crises for the administration. Finally, and most important for the middle school, it structures a thoughtful process whereby the philosophy of education can grow and intersect the planning process over time.

Beginning to Change

The starting point in the CMP is the formation of a management group that can start the ball rolling in the district. The group will generally be made up of six to eight people who have the authority to guide curriculum development (assistant superintendent for instruction, director of secondary education, director of elementary education, etc.). The role of the management team in the conversion process will be to serve as a liaison between the board (and superintendent) and the various committees charged with designing and implementing middle schools. This role will be defined in terms of policy formation, general planning management, resource allocation, and policy implementation.

The primary tasks of the management team, initially, are (1) to agree on a working definition of the term "middle school"; (2) to establish a committee structure that will enable full citizen and professional input into the planning process; and (3) to conduct a preliminary needs assessment that will inform the board of the status of the current intermediate program.

Definitions of the middle school are plentiful and should allow the management team to adopt a set of words rather quickly. The reader should note, however, that the words chosen by the management team and adopted by the board will govern behavior in the committee process. If district personnel do not really believe in the uniqueness of preadolescents, for instance, they should study the literature before endorsing that notion.

Key committees should be formed by both nomination of management team members and solicitations from the field. The committee concept affirms the wisdom of shared decision making and the value of both public and professional input at the policy formation stage. Committee members will, ultimately, go out and sell the concept to those who will be affected by it. The major committees are as follows:

Coordinating committee—a select committee of 15-20 members (citizens and school personnel) who will oversee the entire process during a three- to five-year period. This committee will ensure that the conversion process is smooth and will use a management plan, four primary committees, and a series of other ad hoc groups to accomplish its tasks.

Design committee—consisting of about ten members, who will establish general specifications for the middle school. These standards will be the product of information from a needs assessment as well as input from the public and professional literature.

Program development committee—consisting of about 20 members, who will translate the standards of the design committee into quality indicators for all areas of the middle school curriculum. Specific ad hoc subcommittees in subject areas and special programs will be formed to assist this committee.

Staff development committee—consisting of about ten members, who will plan and recommend inservice training for all middle school teachers charged with carrying out this plan at the classroom level. The basis of inservice planning will be the needs assessment, the program design, and local school implementation plans.

Evaluation committee—consisting of five to seven members, including key evaluation personnel from the district, who will monitor the progress of the conversion plan during the three to five years and report on that progress periodically to the board. Major reports will be:

1. a definition of the middle school, formation of committees, results of the needs assessment, and a schedule for conversion;
2. the middle school design and schedule of events for committees;
3. a fully redefined curriculum complete with standards for all subjects and program areas;
4. a staff development plan based on the projected curriculum;
5. a management plan for implementing the new program.

The third task of the management team, during its early months of planning, is to gather data to assist the committees in planning for the new program. This needs assessment is the subject of the following chapter.

Figure 1. A Sample Philosophy/Goal Statement

The middle school offers a balanced, comprehensive, and success-oriented curriculum. The middle school is a sensitive, caring, supportive learning environment that will provide those experiences that will assist in making the transition from late childhood to adolescence, thereby helping each individual to bridge the gap between the self-contained structure of the elementary school and the departmental structure of the high school.

The middle school curriculums are more exploratory in nature than the elementary school and less specialized than the high school. Realizing that the uniqueness of individual subject disciplines must be recognized, an emphasis on interdisciplinary curriculum development will be stressed. Curriculum programs should emphasize the natural relationship among academic disciplines that facilitate cohesive learning experiences for middle school students through integrative themes, topics, and units. Interdisciplinary goals should overlap subject area goals and provide for interconnections such as reasoning, logical and critical thought, coping capacities, assuming self-management, promoting positive personal development, and stimulating career awareness.

The academic program of a middle school emphasizes skills development through science, social studies, reading, mathematics, and language arts courses. A well-defined skills continuum is used as the basic guide in all schools in each area including physical education, health, guidance, and other educational activities. Exploratory opportunities are provided through well-defined and structured club programs, activity programs, and special interest courses, thereby creating opportunities for students to interact socially, to experience democratic living, to explore areas not in the required curriculum, to do independent study and research, to develop and practice responsible behavior, and to experience working with varying age groups.

The middle school curriculum will be a program of planned learning experiences for our students. The three major components for our middle school curriculum are (1) subject content, (2) personal development, and (3) essential skills.

2
Setting the Stage for Meaningful Change

A BASIC PREMISE OF ALL CURRICULUM DEVELOPMENT IS THAT GOOD decisions are based on good information. This is especially critical in the middle school since, by definition, it is a program designed to meet the needs of preadolescents. A preliminary step in the development of sound middle school programs is gathering good planning information through a thorough needs assessment.

Some districts attempt to convert traditional junior high school programs into middle school curriculums without an analysis of the present condition. This is an error that is almost guaranteed to doom the new effort, because without such an analysis the middle school can only be considered a modification of the junior high school. Nothing could be further from the truth. Whereas the junior high is modeled on the traditional programs of the senior high school (content curriculum), the middle school starts with the learner as the source of design activities (human development). The middle school is *not* a modified junior high school, but rather a more complex and comprehensive educational design.

An early analysis of need can fulfill three key design functions: It can assist in the conceptualization of a new program; it can provide a baseline of information about present conditions for purposes of evaluation; it can give definition to programmatic considerations as the middle school unfolds over time.

In the CMP, the management team initiates the assessment process (gathering baseline data and forming committees) and controls it until a representative coordinating committee is formed. Once formed, the coordinating committee oversees the collection and assembly of planning data from the various sources. At a time in the future, this assembled data will be turned over to a design committee for final analysis and the extraction of meaning for middle schools.

Certain generic questions structure the first data gathering efforts: What is the present status of intermediate education? Where do we seem to be heading in adopting a middle school philosophy? Where do we begin in the conversion to a true middle school? In order to gain a true picture of the present conditions it is necessary to solicit input from all those who are familiar with and involved in middle school programs; teachers, parents, students, and administrators. Two types of data are solicited for early planning: baseline data from district records and projective data based on the perceptions of these various groups.

The importance of true participation at this stage cannot be understated since all subsequent actions by the district will be rationalized by this internal assessment. It is vitally important that district leaders communicate the seriousness of this effort through proper channels. An example of such communication can be found in the superintendent's letter shown in Figure 2, p. 15.

The design and administration of the needs assessment will take many forms. While the amount of data gathered can be brief or extensive, it should clearly contribute to the body of data that planners will need to design a program and bring about meaningful change. Specifically, this data will be used to clarify values, sharpen the conceptualization of a middle school, and reduce philosophic generalities to specific decision-making issues. An outline of the type of data that might be gathered is found in Figure 3, and sample instruments are provided in Appendix A.

An example of how these planning data can be used to assist in the conceptualization of change is provided in Figure 4. Here, a mass of statistical data from achievement testing is reduced to a simple graph that compares student performance with national norms. The reader (and school board members) will quickly note that achievement drops off substantially in all areas in the middle grades. Various kinds of summaries can be prepared from this baseline data that show for all to see the existing conditions that should be addressed in planning (Figure 5).

Development of the projective "opinionnaires" under the CMP utilizes the percentage consensus approach. What planners are looking for is where all groups share common values that can undergird an educational design. Questionnaires are thus set up to solicit such agreement by grouping "percentages" of response to questionnaire items on a Likert scale. In the example shown in Figure 6, teachers and principals in the East Baton Rouge, Louisiana, School District were asked to react to certain characteristics of middle schools as reported in the literature. In item 10, a central philosophic question is asked about whether this middle school should be more child-centered than subject-centered. About 83 percent of the respondents felt that it is important for the middle school to be child centered.

As this type of input is collected, a pattern of response emerges. When the information is turned over to a design committee, the major ideas and concepts that are widely supported are available for planning and incorporation into the educational design. Thus, prior to making any change, the design committee knows the actual status of the present program and, from the surveys, what types of change are desired by those who will be affected by any redesign efforts in moving to middle schools. In terms of change theory, the stronger the consensus, the safer the move forward. Such a technique can also identify, in advance, the possible "tripwires" for the board, superintendent, or even for a building principal (by extracting key data school-by-school).

In contrast to this procedure under the CMP, many school districts "guess" about public opinion and run the risk of being challenged for "imposing" a middle school on the district. Instead of being able to back up their decisions with statistical data, as they might by following the CMP model, many districts simply hope for the best as they forge ahead in the development of middle schools. The CMP procedure clearly tells the district where they really are, what is really involved in moving toward a middle school design, and even where they might safely begin to change the design of their intermediate education programs.

As the design committee presents to the board a philosophy, a set of goals, and major ideas of a sound middle school program—all based on good planning data—the process enters a new phase under the leadership of yet another independent group known as the program development committee. It is the task of this broadly-based group to take the board-adopted design and translate existing programs to that image. Stated another way, the program development committee will rework the existing curriculum to meet the established design parameters. The curriculum will be "mapped out" and reorganized during this stage, and the resources needed to accomplish the various changes will become concrete. How this process of changing is conducted in a school district is the subject of the following chapter.

Figure 2. Sample Letter to Parents

Dear Parent(s):

The Orange County Public School System is currently working to design and implement a sound educational program for middle school students, those in grades 6-8. We feel strongly that parents must be a part of that development.

On the reverse side of this letter is a Middle School Opinionnaire, which lists some ideas that could be included in a middle school. Please complete the opinionnaire according to directions and return it in the stamped, self-addressed envelope by May 25. It is essential that there be a good return rate of the opinionnaire to ensure that the results are meaningful. Your assistance in this effort will be greatly appreciated.

If you have more than one child in grades 6, 7, or 8, please respond to the statements keeping in mind the child whose name appears at the top of this letter. The information you submit will aid us in designing a truly effective middle school program for students. Should you have questions or need further information, please contact John Meinecke, program consultant for the intermediate unit, at 442-3200, extension 379.

Sincerely,

James L. Schott
Superintendent

Figure 3. Outline of Baseline and Projective Data to Be Gathered in Needs Assessment

Baseline Data (Where are we now?)

1. Existing conditions
   a. average daily attendance
   b. absences per teacher per month
   c. number of low socioeconomic students
   d. student mobility
   e. corporal punishment patterns
   f. grade distribution patterns
   g. achievement analyses
   h. teacher, student, parent attitudes toward present program
   i. follow-up survey of junior high graduates
   j. teacher training and certification patterns

2. Existing resources
   a. condition of facilities
   b. analysis of instructional materials
   c. community resources for education

Projective Data (Where do we want to go?)

1. Attitude scales
   a. parent attitudes and opinions
   b. teacher attitudes and opinion
   c. administrator attitudes and opinion
   d. student instructional preference patterns

2. Program definition
   a. student self-concept ratings
   b. teacher skills checklist
   c. values surveys

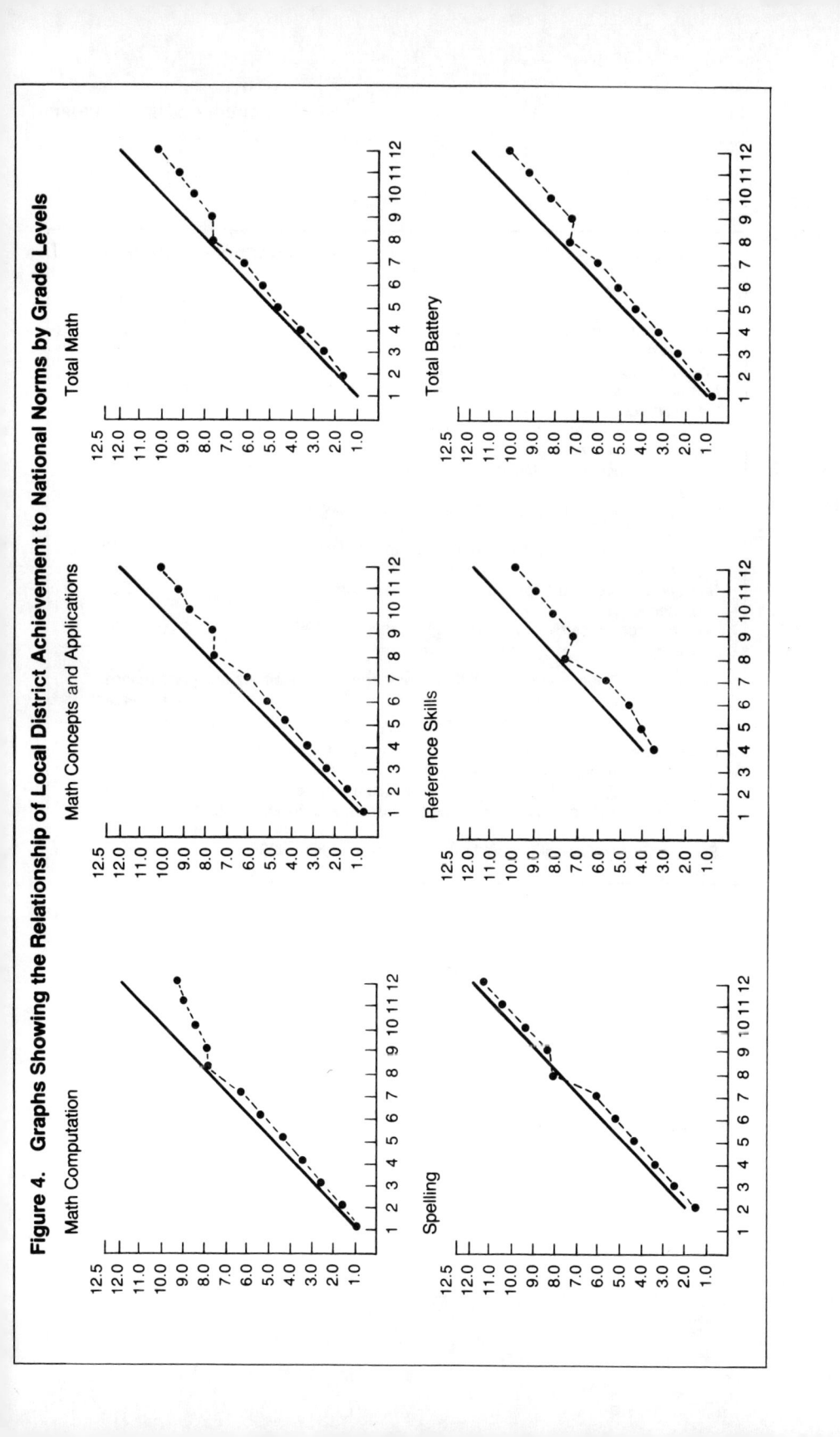

Figure 4. Graphs Showing the Relationship of Local District Achievement to National Norms by Grade Levels

Figure 5. Baseline Summary of Existing Conditions in District

	Low	High
Enrollment range in junior high schools	670	1389
Average daily attendance (May 1984) in junior high schools	83%	95%
Absences per teacher per month in junior high schools	.36	1.27
Number of low socioeconomic students in junior high school as a percentage	11%	56%
Ratio of gifted students to other exceptional education students in junior high school	1/104	179/63
Number of students moving in or out of junior high school during year	33%	70%
Number of students in junior high school experiencing corporal punishment	44	619
Number of students in junior high school experiencing suspension	37	240
Number of students dropping out of junior high school in academic year	0	22
Average score of students in junior high school on CTBS total battery	36	80

Findings: These data confirm that a wide range of conditions and performance exists in the junior high schools of Orange County. The single greatest variable reflected in these data is variance in student population.

Implications: These statistics suggest that the quality of intermediate programs experienced in Orange County may depend upon the individual school. Efforts should be made to equalize programs and performance of the individual schools during the transition to middle schools.

Source: Orange County School District, Orlando, Florida, 1985.

Figure 6. A Sample Opinionnaire with Likert Scale Response

Middle School Opinionnaire (Principal-Teacher Form A)

Please rate each of the following statements in terms of *their importance to you for the middle school*. Choose the answer that tells how you feel about each one and blacken the bubble below the letter of that choice on the separate computer answer sheet. *Use a Number 2 pencil only.* Use the following key to show your feelings.

A	B	C	D	E
Very Important	Important	Fairly Important	Not Very Important	Not Important At All

1. Specialized guidance and counseling services should be available.
2. Both teachers and counselors should be involved in guidance.
3. Emphasis should be on group guidance.
4. Emphasis should be on individual guidance.
5. Each student should have at least one teacher who knows him or her personally.
6. Each student should meet with that teacher individually.
7. Opportunities for social activities for students (dances, athletic games, boosters, etc.) should be provided.
8. Club activities should be scheduled during the day to provide opportunities for group work in areas of common interest.
9. School-wide opportunities should be provided to help students develop good attitudes and standards for themselves.
10. The middle school program should be more child-centered than subject-matter centered.
11. The middle school program should be a unique program bridging the gap between the elementary schools and the secondary schools.
12. Provisions should be made for students to explore their individual interests through exploratory elective courses.
13. Provisions should be made for short-term exploratory/enrichment activities in addition to the regularly scheduled electives.
14. Behavior problems of students should be handled, when possible, by teachers and parents without the involvement of the administrators.
15. An alternative program to suspension should be provided for students having behavior problems (In-school Suspension Program).

3
Designing Middle School Programs for Success

AN ERROR COMMONLY MADE IN MIDDLE SCHOOL PROGRAM DEVELOPMENT is to leave the "design" hanging in the form of generalities. If, for instance, middle schools are to assist learners in the transition from elementary to high school, how is this to be done? Teachers cannot be asked to infer what such generalities mean; they must be spelled out clearly and concisely if the educational design is to accomplish its objectives.

In the CMP model, the coordinating committee guides the process using ad hoc committees that prepare choices for the school board. These choices are presented as progress reports that the board accepts and endorses. It is expected that debate will occur on some points, but such professional dialogue is healthy and gives direction to subsequent activities. An initial progress report may look like the one in Figure 7, p. 23. Other progress reports become more detailed.

If the design committee has done its work properly, it can present the board with a series of documents that collectively define the middle school program to be developed. Each of these documents would provide greater detail as a "deductive logic" takes over in planning. If the board wants this kind of a program (found in the philosophy and goals), then the program would look like what appears in these emerging documents.

In Figure 8, for instance, the three parts of the philosophy statement are broken down into subjects or topics to be found in the new curriculum. In Figure 9, the subject content column of Figure 8 is presented in greater detail to show what is to be taught and when. In Figure 10, the area of developmental physical education is defined by some indicators (to be called standards) of what would be found in that area. Paralleling these curricular documents are certain organization documents that would tell the board about general organization (Figure 11), a proposed schedule (Figure 12), facility changes (Figure 13), and proposed staffing patterns (Figure 14). Each of these documents, which are developed by various subgroups of the program development committee for board approval, can quickly be converted into resource requirements and task sheets by the central staff. Thus, as the board reviews and approves the proposed changes to the middle school curriculum, work can begin.

These many emerging and dissolving committees, and their work in so many areas, may seem overwhelming for any school district. Several observations are in order on this point. First, it must be remembered that the CMP utilizes ad hoc committees so that any one individual would have only a brief time commitment by participation. Second, the CMP allows anyone who wishes to participate in the definition of the program in the area in which they work. No one can claim that they weren't consulted or that outsiders have redefined their area. Third, and perhaps most important from our experience, this procedure all but eliminates special pleading when it gets down to real change at the school level. The board adopts a philosophy, a design, and some program standards for each area. The only question for a department or a teacher is, "How can I meet this expectation in my teaching?" Instruction is a subset of the curriculum!

The number of committees needed to "put meat on the bones" will vary from district to district. Figure 15 lists the ad hoc committees employed by the program development committee in a district with 20 middle schools.

Often the establishment of a middle school program means a grade level conversion from 7-8-9 to 6-7-8. This means that the existing curriculum of the 6th grade in the elementary school must be wedded to the 7th and 8th grade curriculums from the intermediate program. Because most school districts are organized by elementary and secondary divisions, this process can be complex. Certainly, the composition of the program development committee and subcommittees should reflect this reality.

To accomplish this translation of curriculum design into instructional activities, the authors use a modified curriculum-mapping process that requires subject-area committees to clearly identify their purpose (in terms of the board design), their standards of excellence, and how the area will help teach the general learning skills taught throughout the school. (Figure 16 is an example of a worksheet used to give uniformity to this process.)

Having defined the purpose of an area in terms of the board's design for middle schools, the committee then outlines its program on a worksheet that arranges the 6-7-8 time frame by grading periods. In districts where grades are given each nine weeks, the middle school can be thought of as 12 consecutive quarters.

Each nine-week sheet spells out what is to be taught (content and skills) and why (concepts that organize selection of content and skills). In addition, a district may want to correlate this information with various standardized testing skills. At a future date, it is possible to place such an organized curriculum on a school-based computer to monitor the instructional efficiency of the curriculum.

If nothing else were done in establishing middle schools, this mapping experience would be worth the effort. Gaps and redundancy in the curriculum are eliminated. Teaching and testing are coordinated. Teachers are asked to rationalize their choice of content in terms of what they want students to learn. Finally, the establishment of a timeframe for covering subject matter allows for a horizontal look across the curriculum that will later simplify interdisciplinary efforts.

As the new curriculum comes into focus, the need for special instructional materials and facility modifications are noted and forwarded to the program development committee for compilation and analysis (example: do we need science laboratories in the 6th grade?).

Another by-product of such work is the realization by participants that there is more to do in daily instruction but without additional time. This "puzzle of the middle school," more than any other single act, reveals the new philosophy to teachers. The middle school curriculum cannot be a mastery curriculum; it is exploratory and comprehensive, and there is a balance among the many parts. Teachers who map their subjects will suddenly understand the logic of the block-of-time schedule and the use of interdisciplinary teams of teachers.

This input from the various members of the many committees under the CMP helps to build an educated advocacy group whose members can explain the emerging program at their school. While it is our experience that this process will generate sincere excitement among even veteran teachers, there will also be some genuine apprehension and fundamental concerns such as (1) Where will I fit into this new program? (2) What if I don't possess the skills to be a middle school teacher? These questions, and others, are the subject of the next chapter.

Figure 7. Initial Board Report

MIDDLE SCHOOL PROGRESS REPORT

Philosophy: The middle school operates within the general policy guidelines of the Orange County Public Schools.

The Middle School:

- provides unique experiences for students in transition between childhood and adolescence
- helps students become proficient in the basic skills
- helps students develop fundamental thinking processes which foster independent learning
- helps meet the special physical, social, emotional, and character needs of preadolescent students.

Our Beginnings: In order to oversee the comprehensive planning and development of 19 middle schools in Orange County, a coordinating committee made up of community and school district leaders was formed in the fall of 1984. The committee's charge is to coordinate the efforts of numerous standing and ad hoc committees related to the implementation of a middle school design. This coordinating committee has met four times (September 13, October 2, November 13, and December 3, 1984).

Present Status: The design committee has developed quality control standards for all middle school facilities, curriculum, and instructional programs. The attached report was submitted December 12, 1984.

The evaluation committee is an ongoing committee whose purpose is to monitor and assess all progress and achievement in the conversion to middle schools. That report was presented at the school board work session December 12, 1984.

Future Tasks: The standards, as developed by the design committee, will become the foundation upon which a comprehensive, successful middle school program will be built.

The next immediate step involves the appointment of the program development and staff development committees. The program development committee's task is to organize and monitor ad hoc committees covering each component of the middle school plan.

The staff development committee's task is to organize a comprehensive inservice plan to prepare all middle school personnel in order to successfully implement the programs and organization.

Next progress report—late spring 1985.

Figure 11. Proposed General Organization Standards

The organization of the middle school is such that a smooth transition may be made from the self-contained classroom of the elementary school to the departmentalized high school. Provision is made to meet the unique social, academic, and personal needs of children as they emerge from childhood into adolescence. Flexibility in time utilization, and in the grouping of students and teachers, is provided to allow for balanced instruction.

1. Teacher grouping
   - Teachers are organized into interdisciplinary teams to provide instruction in the core subjects of reading, language arts, science, mathematics, and social studies.
   - The interdisciplinary team serves a common group of students.
   - The interdisciplinary team controls a block of time.
   - The members of the interdisciplinary team are assigned classrooms in close proximity to one another.
   - The members of the interdisciplinary team have a common planning period.
   - A member of the interdisciplinary team shall be designated as team leader.

2. Student grouping
   - The students are organized by grade levels.
   - Each grade level is divided into teams of approximately 90 to 135 students as is compatible with the interdisciplinary instructional team.
   - Provision is made for instruction at differing ability levels, at differing skills levels, and in different interest areas.

3. Time
   - Provision is made for a flexible daily time schedule.
   - A block of time equivalent to five 45-minute time segments (225 minutes) is assigned to the interdisciplinary team for academic instruction.
   - A 90-minute block of time is provided for exploration and physical education activities.

Figure 12. Proposed Middle School Student Schedule

25 min A/A	225 min Academic Block	25 min Lunch	45 min Enrich.	45 min P.E.	25 min Passing

The day schedule contains:
   7—45-minute periods
   1—25-minute A/A period
   1—25-minute lunch period
   passing times (total of 25 minutes)

   Total student day of 6 hours 30 minutes

   *Other patterns may be suggested

Figure 7. Initial Board Report

MIDDLE SCHOOL PROGRESS REPORT

Philosophy: The middle school operates within the general policy guidelines of the Orange County Public Schools.

The Middle School:

- provides unique experiences for students in transition between childhood and adolescence
- helps students become proficient in the basic skills
- helps students develop fundamental thinking processes which foster independent learning
- helps meet the special physical, social, emotional, and character needs of preadolescent students.

Our Beginnings: In order to oversee the comprehensive planning and development of 19 middle schools in Orange County, a coordinating committee made up of community and school district leaders was formed in the fall of 1984. The committee's charge is to coordinate the efforts of numerous standing and ad hoc committees related to the implementation of a middle school design. This coordinating committee has met four times (September 13, October 2, November 13, and December 3, 1984).

Present Status: The design committee has developed quality control standards for all middle school facilities, curriculum, and instructional programs. The attached report was submitted December 12, 1984.

The evaluation committee is an ongoing committee whose purpose is to monitor and assess all progress and achievement in the conversion to middle schools. That report was presented at the school board work session December 12, 1984.

Future Tasks: The standards, as developed by the design committee, will become the foundation upon which a comprehensive, successful middle school program will be built.

The next immediate step involves the appointment of the program development and staff development committees. The program development committee's task is to organize and monitor ad hoc committees covering each component of the middle school plan.

The staff development committee's task is to organize a comprehensive inservice plan to prepare all middle school personnel in order to successfully implement the programs and organization.

Next progress report—late spring 1985.

Figure 8. An Outline of Proposed Curriculum

Program Areas

Subject Content	Personal Development	Essential Skills
3 years Math 3 years Science 3 years Communication/ Language Arts 3 years Social Studies 3 years Reading 3 years Developmental P.E. 3 years Exploratory Courses	Advisor/Advisee Program Developmental P.E. Health and Nutrition Individual Growth Social Growth Citizenship Creativity Mini Courses Special Interests	School Awareness Community Awareness Reading Listening Speaking Writing Vocabulary Thinking Problem Solving Decision Making Study Media Map Reference Test Taking Computer Literacy Computation and/or Calculator

Figure 9. Proposed Subject Content

Students experience learning through a program emphasizing the integration of the *five* major subject content areas: reading, language arts, math, science, and social studies. The specifics of what we want students to learn and how we help them learn those things are central to instructional content and process. Curriculum organization, sequencing, instructional methods, teaching styles, and student learning styles are all central aspects of subject content. Through a well-integrated program designed to meet their needs, our students will develop an appreciation for a well-balanced, comprehensive, core curriculum.

The core curriculum consists of the following:

1. Three years of math
2. Three years of science (life science, earth science, and physical science)
3. Three years of communication/language arts (reading, writing, speaking)
4. Three years of social studies (study of U.S., civics, Florida history, geography)
5. Three years of reading (developmental, content area, remedial)
6. Three years of exploratory courses in these areas:
    a. academic (foreign language, computer literacy)
    b. practical arts/vocational ed. (home economics, business ed., industrial arts, agriculture, public service, health ed., distributive ed.)
    c. fine arts (drama, speech, art, music)
7. Three years of developmental P.E. (regularly scheduled as determined by school district).

Figure 10. Sample Definition of Subject Area

DEVELOPMENTAL PHYSICAL EDUCATION—The physical education program provides fitness activities that are enjoyable and developmental while stressing motor skills, good sportsmanship, and the interdependency of the body and mind that are essential for a natural part of healthful living. Middle schoolers need to understand and respect their bodies, minds, and environment. Important components of a physical education program include:

- Life sports as a part of the three-year program.
- Health and safety instruction provided at each grade level for each P.E. activity.
- Individual and group activities that provide opportunities for students to demonstrate skills in healthy competition.
- Provisions for students with physical limitations and disabilities (adaptive P.E. programs).
- Intramural activities as a natural outgrowth of the physical education department.
- The development of motor skills.
- Fitness-level testing each year that allows students to assess their own fitness development. Strategies for self-improvement are possible because the program provides a knowledge of body functions during activities and also information concerning physical training.
- Interaction and coordination with other disciplines in the school curriculum.

Figure 11. Proposed General Organization Standards

The organization of the middle school is such that a smooth transition may be made from the self-contained classroom of the elementary school to the departmentalized high school. Provision is made to meet the unique social, academic, and personal needs of children as they emerge from childhood into adolescence. Flexibility in time utilization, and in the grouping of students and teachers, is provided to allow for balanced instruction.

1. Teacher grouping
   - Teachers are organized into interdisciplinary teams to provide instruction in the core subjects of reading, language arts, science, mathematics, and social studies.
   - The interdisciplinary team serves a common group of students.
   - The interdisciplinary team controls a block of time.
   - The members of the interdisciplinary team are assigned classrooms in close proximity to one another.
   - The members of the interdisciplinary team have a common planning period.
   - A member of the interdisciplinary team shall be designated as team leader.

2. Student grouping
   - The students are organized by grade levels.
   - Each grade level is divided into teams of approximately 90 to 135 students as is compatible with the interdisciplinary instructional team.
   - Provision is made for instruction at differing ability levels, at differing skills levels, and in different interest areas.

3. Time
   - Provision is made for a flexible daily time schedule.
   - A block of time equivalent to five 45-minute time segments (225 minutes) is assigned to the interdisciplinary team for academic instruction.
   - A 90-minute block of time is provided for exploration and physical education activities.

Figure 12. Proposed Middle School Student Schedule

25 min A/A	225 min Academic Block	25 min Lunch	45 min Enrich.	45 min P.E.	25 min Passing

The day schedule contains:
7—45-minute periods
1—25-minute A/A period
1—25-minute lunch period
passing times (total of 25 minutes)

Total student day of 6 hours 30 minutes

*Other patterns may be suggested

Figure 13. Proposed Facilities Standards

The instructional program and the organizational pattern of the middle school dictate the facility requirements. The facilities should allow for varied instructional experiences, support the middle school concept, and meet the personnel and support-staff needs.

1. Essential considerations
   - Increased attractiveness by use of color schemes and graphics.
   - Adequate instructional space and equipment for each curricular program.
   - Clustered interdisciplinary team instruction rooms.
   - Team planning/work/conference area.
   - Flexible classroom space.
   - Computer instruction area.
   - Alternative education area.
   - Clinic area.
   - Closeable restroom stalls for boys and girls.
   - Adequate area for physical education and recreational activities.
   - Appropriate private shower and changing facilities for boys and girls.
   - Appropriate exceptional education/student services.

2. Desirable considerations
   - In-house television capability.
   - Adequate acoustical treatment (ceiling tile, floor covering, etc.)

Note:

Existing science facilities are clustered posing difficulties in the adjacent team room concept. It is suggested that the sixth grade science program be taught in convenient classrooms which are equipped with a water source, portable lab facility, storage, and student stations at tables. Seventh and eighth grade science classes should be taught in existing science rooms at the expense of being removed from the team area.

Any new facility or any major renovation of an existing facility should address the decentralization of science rooms.

Figure 14. Proposed Organization Standards For Staffing

An effective middle school is dependent upon professional and nonprofessional staff who possess special understandings, skills, and attitudes in working with middle school students, parents, and community members. An effective middle school staff supports, understands the need for, and implements the middle school concept. These personnel see the middle school as neither elementary nor secondary, but as an institution designed to meet the special need of emerging adolescents. The school-wide philosophy should be student-centered, not subject-centered. Each staff member's role is to help all students develop emotionally, socially, and academically. Recommended administrative staffing pattern (school of 1,200 students):

1. ADMINISTRATIVE STAFF
   a. One principal
   b. Two assistant principals

2. SUPPORT STAFF
   a. Three grade coordinators (10-month with provisions for extended contract)
   b. Guidance counselors; recommended counselor/student ratio is 1 to 350
      Note: Special consideration given for additional staffing for exceptional education centers housed at some schools.

   c. Media
   d. Alternative education
   e. Nurses
   f. Aides
   g. Psychologist
   h. Social worker
   i. Police liaison
   j. Additions (school volunteers)

3. TEACHERS
   a. Team teachers
   b. Exploratory ed. teachers
   c. Exceptional ed. teachers

Figure 15. Types of Ad Hoc Subcommittees under Program Development

Agriculture	Language Arts
Alternative Education	Language Arts ESOL
Art	Language Learning Disabilities
Autistic	Library/Media
Business Education	Marketing
Career Education	Mathematics
Computer Education	Music
Educable Mentally Handicapped	Physical Education
Emotionally Handicapped	Physically Impaired
Extracurricular	Physical/Occupational Therapy
Foreign Language	Public Service
Gifted Education	Severely Emotionally Disturbed
Health	Severely Emotionally Handicapped
Hearing Impaired	Science
Home Economics	Social Studies
Industrial Arts	Specific Learning Disabilities
Intramurals	Student Services
Itinerant Speech/Language	Visually Impaired

Figure 16. Mapping Worksheet with Standards

Curriculum Area: *Computer Education*

Purpose: The overall goal in the educational use of computers is to integrate computer literacy into all content areas of the middle school curriculum, thus providing an additional tool for interdisciplinary curriculum development. In addition, elective computer courses in application and programming provide for personal development and the reinforcement of essential skills.

Program Descriptors	Yes	No	Action Plan to Achieve
1. Microcomputers, either permanently located in all classrooms or on mobile carts, are available for classroom use.			
2. Additional mobile computers will be available to move into classrooms when necessary or to develop a mini lab when desired.			
3. Each school will have at least two qualified full-time computer education teachers.			
4. Each school will have at least two complete computer labs containing a minimum of 16 microcomputers and have a ratio of 2 students per computer. Each lab shall include necessary computer-system hardware, software, and peripheral equipment to meet current and future trends and developments. The complete computer lab will consist of necessary space, lighting, seating, air cooling system, electrical system, and security plus access to telecommunications.			
5. Daily lab schedules should include time set aside for independent student use.			
6. All students in grades 6 and 7 will be scheduled into one of the computer labs for a minimum of 3 hours a week in order to meet the state requirements for computer literacy.			
7. A minimum of two computers with needed peripherals will be located in the teachers' work area for teacher use; i.e., grade recording, software review, word processing, etc.			

Note: The Computer Literacy Program for the 6th and 7th grade should be interdisciplinary and taught through the team concept.

Both the media center and the administrative offices have needs for computerization of their functions. These noninstructional needs should be addressed by the appropriate middle school ad hoc committee.

Essential Skills:
(Skills reinforced regardless of discipline or program spiral)

Reading	Problem-solving	Computer literacy
Listening	Decision-making	Computation or calculation
Writing	Thinking	Motor
Vocabulary		

4
People Make Middle Schools Work

AS THE PROGRAM DEVELOPMENT COMMITTEE COMPLETES ITS WORK, THE board acquires the written middle school curriculum that it mandated. En route, many people have been directly involved in the analysis and design of the program. The rationale, philosophy, goals, and program standards should be understood by those groups who will be affected by the program (students, parents, teachers, and administrators). Still, it is an intended curriculum, not a delivered curriculum. The difference between the two is usually staff development!

Most intermediate teachers, due to certification patterns, are trained in secondary education. The secondary focus on subject content at the university level usually means that depth of understanding is in one area. By contrast, elementary-trained teachers have coursework in all major subject areas and, recently, a heavy emphasis on individualizing to meet differences in human development. The exhibit that follows illustrates the degree of flexibility in 6th grade classes when compared to 7th and 8th grade classes in one district.

Since districts do not have the luxury of hiring a new staff for the middle school, additional training must be provided. Staff development can be expensive, so it is important that inservice be tied directly to the skills and understanding needed to implement the planned curriculum. All too often, middle school staff development is nothing more than entertainment or practice in unrelated teaching techniques.

The final ad hoc committee is the staff development committee, formed as the program development committee finalizes its findings. Its major purpose is to prepare middle school personnel to implement the program mandated by the board. Specifically, this committee should identify staff development needs, develop a plan for meeting these needs, and schedule the proposed inservice to accomplish the task within the board's time frame.

Those responsible for middle school staff development need to be wary of targeting only teachers for inservice. Because of the philosophical change required to implement the middle school, a comprehensive plan is more appropriate (secretaries can also contribute to climate). In the following exhibits, a set of recommendations, a training program, and a sample schedule of events are provided for study.

The other chief concern of the staff development committee is the direct welfare of the teaching staff in moving to middle schools. Most staff are threatened by change, and such concerns should be identified using instruments like the Concerns-Based Adoption Model (CBAM) developed by the Research Development Center for Teacher Education at the University of Texas. (Sample concerns are shown in Figure 22.)

Finally, each district must take steps to make the middle school teacher feel as special as the students they teach. Historically, the junior high school failed because, among other things, there were no trained teachers for the junior high. Middle schools, after 20 years, have largely failed to change the elementary-secondary organization of most state education departments and are forced to "go it alone."

Some districts have begun to recognize the special set of skills needed by middle school teachers and provide some form of internal certification. This may be a simple recognition of training (see Figure 23) or a novel category of teacher with special privileges such as selective placement or closed corridors to administrative roles. Whatever is done by the local district, it must be recognized that the success of the middle school depends on its teachers.

The *actions* of all of the various committees under the CMP require organization if their work is to bring results. The final chapter speaks of that management and of the bottom line—evaluation.

Figure 17. The Subject Area Mapped by Nine-Week Period

Curriculum Area: Computer Education   Grade Level: 6

Subject: Basic Literacy   Grading Period: First Nine Weeks

Major Topics/Content	Generalizations/Concepts	Intended Outcomes	Specific Skills/Standards	SA	PS
General Function and Capabilities of Computer System	A computerized society requires that all students need to develop an awareness and functional working knowledge of computers.	Recognize the general makeup and function of computers.	Identify the parts of a computer system, including hardware and software.		X
			Identify the purpose of the components of a computer system, including both hardware and software.		X X
			Use appropriate terms in reference to computers.		X X X
			Explain how a computer works.		X X
			Recognize the capabilities of different types of computers.		X
Computer Operations		Follow directions related to computer interaction.	Follow verbal and written directions.		
			Respond appropriately to directions given by a computer program.		X
		Develop keyboard skills.	Identify and use numbers and letters on keyboard.		X
			Identify and use common special purpose keys.		X X X

Check Test

Figure 18. Comparing What is Seen in 6th Grade vs. 7th and 8th Grade Classrooms

Observable item	Percentage 6th	Percentage 7th-8th
Student work displayed	70	51
Seats other than rows	60	28
Living objects in room	61	34
Frequent praise by teacher	70	59
Student doing independent work	47	29
Learning centers present	37	12
Student work folders used	42	30
Still continuum cards in use	67	19
Small group instruction in use	48	27
Grouping/regrouping for instruction	64	27
Student contracts used	26	18

Source: *Things Principals See* (Wiles and Bondi 1985)

Figure 19. Rationale and Recommendations for Middle School Staff Development

A traditional value within county schools is that the professional development of all district employees is a never-ending process. It also has been agreed upon that inservice training as reflected in a staff development plan be directly linked to precisely identified employee job-related needs.

Employees' training needs emerge at an accelerated pace whenever the work environment is changed. The district's transition to middle schools will no doubt greatly change the environment for affected employees.

Beyond the practical and philosophical basis for implementing a comprehensive inservice training program is the requirement that the district provide opportunities for instructional employees to earn the appropriate state certification as a teacher at the middle school level.

The middle school staff development committee strongly recommends that all middle school teachers receive inservice training in the middle school topics identified by the PRIME Bill.

The committee recommends that district-level middle school certification be instituted and that preferential placement to middle school teaching positions be linked to this certification.

The committee recommends that individual profile data for potential middle school teachers be gathered as needed from the district's existing data storage/retrieval systems.

The committee endorses leadership training for potential middle school administrators. It is suggested that this training begin as soon as practical after a pool of potential middle school administrators is selected.

The committee recommends that the two consultants and two district-level employees plan training activities consistent with the first recommendation. An initial offering of this training should be delivered to volunteers during the fall of 1985.

The committee recommends that the district level program consultants responsible for the subject/service areas included within the middle school curriculum facilitate the delivery of inservice training to appropriate instructional personnel.

Figure 20. Middle School Training Components

Certification Component (Middle Level Education—Orange County Public Schools Component #20561)

This component will focus on the following topics of study:

1. The middle grades
2. Understanding the middle-grades student
3. Organizing interdisciplinary instruction
4. Curriculum development
5. Developing critical and creative thinking in students
6. Counseling functions of the teacher
7. Developing creative-learning materials
8. Planning and evaluating programs

To meet the requirements of the component, each participant will attend ten two-hour workshops. The program will consist of 30 hours of instruction in a workshop setting and 30 hours of supervised in-school follow-up activities.

It is anticipated that successful completion of this component plus one year of successful teaching in a middle school will lead to middle school certification for the participants.

Leadership for Team Leaders and Grade Coordinators

This training will focus on group process and communication skills that will enhance the ability of team leaders and grade coordinators to carry out their assigned responsibilities. The participants will receive six hours of skills-based training. All participants will be expected to have successfully completed Middle Level Education component prior to attending this training.

Overview of the Middle School

An audio-visual presentation giving an overview of middle level education in Orange County public schools. It addresses the planned structure and curriculum of the middle school.

This will be a one-hour activity.

Program of Instruction

An overview of the instructional program of the middle school. This would cover the subject content, areas of personal development, and essential skills. This activity will be one hour of information with opportunity for participants to ask questions

Middle Level Education for School-Based Administrators

The presentation will be modeled on the certification component (OCPS Component #20561–Middle Level Education) with emphasis in those areas of special interest to the school-level administrator. It will consist of 20 hours of instruction with specified activities to be carried out at the school site.

Selected Topics

This training will include topics from the certification component that meet special needs of those personnel who deal with the middle school child in other than classroom settings. An example of this would be "Understanding the Middle Grades Student" for school secretaries, custodians, and other classified personnel. This would be a one-hour activity.

Source: *The Essential Middle School* (Wiles and Bondi 1986).

Figure 21. Middle School Staff Development and Meetings Schedule, Fall 1985

	AUGUST			SEPTEMBER						OCTOBER								NOVEMBER								DECEMBER					
	22	26	27	5	6	12	13	19	20	26	27	10	11	17	18	24	25	31	1	7	8	14	15	21	22	5	6	10	12	13
Teachers						1		2		3		4		5		6		7		8		9		10						
Leadership Group											1		2				3				5		6		7		6			
Principals										1							2							3			8			
Assistant Principals				1								2						3				4								
Management Team	1												2												3					
School Visits (as needed)						1				2										3						5	6	7	8	
School Board																												1		
Coordinating Committee															1											2				
Staff Development														1																
Grant																1					2		2							
Evaluation Committee											1																3			
Program Consultants				1								2						3				4				5				
Public Relations Committee						1																	2							

Figure 22. Results of Open-Ended Statement of Concern Questionnaire
Middle School Change Process, May 1985
Submitted by Program Evaluation Section

As part of the evaluation of the change process for the transition to middle schools, junior high administrators and a random sample of teachers who work primarily with 7th and 8th grade students recently responded to the Open-Ended Statement of Concern Questionnaire. The questionnaire was developed as part of the Concerns-Based Adoption Model (CBAM) from the Research Development Center for Teacher Education at the University of Texas. The purpose of the questionnaire is to determine the concerns of people who are using or contemplating innovations during the innovation-adoption process. Responses were received from all 19 junior high schools. The following concerns were expressed in response to the question, "When you think about middle school, what are you concerned about? (Do not say what you think others are concerned about, but only what concerns you now.)"

Concerns of Teachers

- Emphasis on strong academic program may be sacrificed with teachers responsible for areas other than academics; lack of attention to basic skills.
- Being part of a team; will the personalities and philosophies of team members allow for cooperation?
- Implementing the advisor–advisee program; further responsibilities in guidance and nonacademic areas in which I have not been trained.
- Lack of knowledge of the advantages of the middle school for this age group; common commitment by administrators and teachers to the middle school concept.
- Training in what the middle school is all about.
- Certification and my assignment responsibilities.
- Consequences of fewer extracurricular activities.
- Dealing with a different age group.
- A feeling of being left out by teachers not in the major four academic areas.

Figure 23

ORANGE COUNTY PUBLIC SCHOOLS

MIDDLE SCHOOL TRAINING CERTIFICATE

FOR SUCCESSFULLY COMPLETING
THE PRESCRIBED COURSE OF STUDY FOR

MIDDLE LEVEL EDUCATION

Given this _____ day of _____ , 19 ____

Superintendent   Deputy Superintendent   Program Consultant
                     for Instruction

5
The Promises Must Be Kept

DURING THE PAST 20 YEARS, THE MIDDLE SCHOOL HAS BEEN A MAJOR innovation in American education. Few persons are unaware of the term middle school, and in many ways the middle school movement has changed the face of intermediate education in this country. On the other hand, a regular and always embarassing question for any middle school consultant is, "Where should I go to see middle schools in action?" In truth, the authors know of no school that could be documented as a middle school; the concept is just too imprecise.

What, then, is a middle school? For the authors, it is a school with a certain set of priorities and purposes that organizes itself to accomplish those goals. Middle schools, compared to junior high schools, are dedicated to serving preadolescents (ages 10-14) through a comprehensive (physical, social, emotional, intellectual, moral) program that is both balanced (no one area dominates the others) and success oriented (all persons experiencing the program continue to develop).

For the middle school to work, it must be defined. Clichés and platitudes about child-centered, humanistic programs with flexible schedules and advisory programs have *not* produced middle schools. Because you can't evaluate what you can't define, evaluation is very important to the middle school. As Gagne has stated, "What one really wants to know about a given curriculum is whether it works."

Everyone has a stake in evaluation. The board should be concerned about the money to be spent; a more complex program costs more money! Both teachers and administrators should be concerned about workloads; a more complex program calls for more work. Parents of middle school children should be concerned about outcomes;

the middle school should deliver benefits without such penalties as dropping achievement scores. Evaluation in the middle school can be useful in five ways:

1. To check on the effectiveness of the program.
2. To validate the operational hypotheses (it will benefit students thusly).
3. To provide information basic to the guidance of students.
4. To provide psychological security to staff and students.
5. To provide the basis of public relations.

In Chapter 2 we suggested that the beginning point for meaningful change was an assessment of need. Data obtained could help establish the present state of things, give direction to changes, and suggest an order to the change process. We prescribed an evaluation committee that might serve in a watchdog role for the board, measuring progress and reporting on events. Without board support, the more expensive, more complex middle school concept will evaporate.

In districts that have taken this data-gathering step, there is little slippage because positive changes can be documented. For example, the board sees both average daily attendance and teacher use of sick-leave days in dollar-and-cents terms. There are some promises that the middle school can keep. Nearly 20 years ago the following middle school evaluation hypotheses were proposed by Vincent Hines:

1. The middle school will provide a rich program of exploratory courses.
2. There will be fewer and less intense social and psychological problems.
3. Students will develop more adequate self-concepts.
4. Students will become more self-directed learners.
5. Graduates will succeed better in high school.
6. There will be less teacher turnover.
7. Teacher morale will be higher.
8. The organization will facilitate better use of individual teacher competencies and skills.
9. Attendance of students will increase.
10. Teachers will use a greater variety of media to meet the diverse needs of preadolescent learners.
11. Patrons (parents, students, teachers) will hold more positive attitudes toward the objectives and procedures.
12. Student achievement on standardized tests will equal or exceed that of students in conventional schools (Wiles and Bondi 1986b).

These 12 items can, in most districts, form the backbone of an evaluation system that measures results. If the middle school can't keep such promises, then why make the effort? In middle schools, evaluation is essential.

Our Curriculum Management Plan attempts to keep all parties informed at all times. Only through such openness can the pervasive logic of the middle school win out over special interests, suspicion, and ignorance. Three key groups for communicating about progress in middle school development are school personnel, the board, and parents.

Initially, school personnel will view the middle school with a certain degree of skepticism because of its previous association with educational innovations. To the degree that the middle school is merely projected as a new schedule, team teaching, or advisory guidance, it will be indistinguishable from all of the other innovations of the past 20 years. Instead, the move to middle schools should be projected as a major curriculum renewal effort affecting nearly one-third of the students in the district.

The process of involving those who will be affected within the committee structure has already been described. This structure should allow all who wish to participate to make their contributions. Literally hundreds of parents, teachers, administrators, and students can have input as the process unfolds.

The management team must work hard to project changes, and the results expected from such change, so that everyone understands and feels at ease with the process. An outline of the complete curriculum cycle and the types of major events is shown in Figure 24, p. 43. A rough schedule of projected events can also be listed quite early so that everyone will have a feel for the time flow of the change process (Figure 25). Finally, as the number of events grows, activity sheets for major events can be developed and projected onto calendars (Figure 26) to be shared by all parties. Computerization of this process is easily achieved.

Certain non-middle school events in the district must also be integrated into the planning for coordination. Examples might be related curriculum change in the high school (the 9th grade moving up), rezoning of students prior to assignment of middle school teachers, and transportation and facility modifications.

Obviously, the board will need a comprehensive picture of the changes underway, along with the decision-making and budgetary implications of each change. As stated earlier, the board sees the process as a distance-rate-time problem dependant upon such variables as available funds and existing facilities. The important thing to remember is that if the board knows where it is going and has a long-range plan to get there, turnover of personnel won't sidetrack the effort.

For the board, the evaluation committee provides a variety of feedback mechanisms. Most important among these are the progress reports delivered each semester (Figure 27). The board should also receive a schedule of events projected over the life of the plan (Figure 28) as well as a semester transition schedule (Figure 29). At the end of each semester the board should be presented with a summary of all activities that have occurred (Figure 30) as well as the accomplishments of those activities (Figure 31). The computer program "Save It" is excellent for these purposes.

The board then will know where planning and development are going, what is to be accomplished, what has been accomplished, and what is coming next. Such information allows the board ample time to plan for budget, personnel, and facilities modifications.

The final group to be kept informed, and the most important group from our perspective, is the parents, who are the school's primary patrons. It can be expected that they will be especially curious about such a major program change. Our Curriculum Management Plan involves parents from the beginning and seeks to keep them informed throughout the process.

In addition to the involvement of key persons from key groups on the various committees, we advocate the formation of a special ad hoc committee on public relations during the second year of conversion. This committee will notify parents of upcoming changes and highlight the positive aspects of the middle school program. The committee's mission (Figure 32), its activities (Figure 33), and the type of information it dispenses need careful consideration. It is particularly important to remember that the logic of the middle school program is backed by surveys showing the degree to which the public desired such a program. As quickly as possible, the public relations effort should focus on the local school level.

In summary, the role of evaluation in developing middle schools is to inform, validate achievements, and sustain the process over time. Historically, the lack of evaluation in middle school development has been an Achilles heel; those who have failed to show the merits of middle school education have not sustained the change process.

A Final Word

Throughout this book we have stressed the process of developing middle schools rather than the substance of a middle school. We have stated that the middle school is, in our opinion, the most exciting educational idea ever conceived in the United States. We have also observed that in many districts, the middle school concept remains undeveloped and undefined.

The middle school movement in this country is quite young, and we believe the future of the middle school in America is quite bright. We sincerely appreciate the support of the Association for Supervision and Curriculum Development in helping to develop this book for its members. It is our hope that 20 years from now ASCD can report to its members that the middle school is flourishing.

Figure 24. The Curriculum Development Cycle Defines Activity

COMPREHENSIVE PLAN OF THE DENVER PUBLIC SCHOOLS

Analysis Stage

1. Identify Denver Public Schools' philosophy.
2. Identify board policy relative to middle schools.
3. Superintendent (public) statement on middle schools.
4. Outline timeframe for implementation.
5. Formation of centralized coordinating group.
6. Delineation of tasks + appointment of subcommittee.
7. Develop "definition" of Denver Middle Schools.
8. Structure awareness/orientation campaign.
   a. Administrators
   b. Teacher groups

Design Stage

9. Translate philosophy into goal statements.
10. Project preliminary budget/resource base.
11. Prioritize goal statements.
12. Translate goal statements to objectives format.
13. Block out 3–5 year plan for implementation.
14. Establish management/information system to monitor progress of implementation (external audit).
15. Establish evaluation targets, time, responsibilities, resources; identify baseline data needed.
16. Conduct needs assessment.
17. Develop final management system (PERT).

Implementation or Management Stage

18. Provide advanced organizers (simple plan) to all interested persons.
19. Provide each school with resource kits, glossaries, data bank from needs assessment (local planning/decision-making data).
20. Formation of teams in each school to serve as:
    a. study group for mapping curriculum/skills
    b. planning group/house plan
    c. team/cooperative teaching unit
21. Provide preliminary staff development (demonstration teaching) in all schools on:
    a. advisor/advisee program
    b. continuous progress curriculums
    c. team planning and teaching
22. Require school-by-school development plan including curriculum, staff development, evaluation, community involvement.
23. Provide local budget supplement based on plan.

Evaluation Stage

24. Conduct formative evaluation (external audit) every six weeks to monitor management outline.
25 Conduct major review after 6 months—revise timeline, goals, needs, etc.
26. Develop master evaluation plan (sum of all schools) for 3-year period.

Source: Authors' notes, Denver, Colorado, 1980.

Figure 25. Sample Schedule of Events

Summer 84

* 100- Assessment of 19 middle school buildings by consultants
200- Working definition developed by management team
201- Committee structure for planning designed
202- Committee members identified
800- Needs assessment conducted/analyzed
900- Board Report I submitted by management team

Fall 84

210- Major committees formed/begin meeting
211- Development of middle school standards
212- Curriculum management plan outlined
810- Evaluation plan developed
811- Link to SDOE funding for middle schools established
812- Initial school profile folders delivered to principals
910- Board Report II delivered by coordinating committee

Spring 85

220- Program development committee formed
221- Curriculum maps developed for all subject areas
222- Special-topics areas studied/recommendations
223- Program development committee sends specifications to staff development
224- Decision on interscholastic sports/recommendations to board
320- Orientation for elementary, junior high, high school administrators and supervisors
420- PR emphasis on planning process (teachers target) emerging design
620- Staff development committee formed
621- List of district and external consultants compiled/computerized
622- Teacher inservice competencies identified
820- Specifications for student evaluation developed/forward to data processing
821- CMP worksheets computerized
822- Instructional assessment summarized for staff development committee
920- Board Report III delivered by Coordinating Committee

Summer 85

130- Facility decisions made according to design specifications (size? closing?)
230- Curriculums adjusted to accommodate Department of Education frameworks
330- Select pool of potential middle school administrators/leaders
331- One-week inservice for middle school administrators
530- Contract issues on assignment, transfer, training teachers studied
930- Board Report IV delivered by CC

Fall 85

140- Facility modifications identified, scheduled 86/87, 87/88
240- Complete curriculum delivered to all teachers
340- Begin seminar series for potential middle school leaders
440- PR emphasis on curriculum (target parents) design
640- Teachers assess own school by new curriculum
740- Resource assessment by building against curriculum needs
741- Total resource budget developed for 86/87, 87/88
840- Data processing pilots new student evaluation in one school
940- Board Report V delivered by Coordinating Committee

Spring 86

450- PR emphasis on program (target PTAs and community groups)
950- Board Report VI

Summer 86

360- Assignment of administrative staff to middle schools
660- Assignment of 7th grade faculty (some 8th) to middle schools
661- Pilot training for admin/7th grade teachers
960- Board Report VII

Fall 86

270- Pilot middle school components in selected schools/7th grade only
470- PR emphasis on services (target 5th/6th grade parents)
770- Develop plans for 6th and 8th grade resource deployment
870- DP student evaluation in place for 7th graders/all schools
970- Board Report VIII

Spring 87

480- PR emphasis on meeting needs (target 5th/6th parents)
680- Assignment of 6th and 8th grade teachers
980- Board Report IX

Summer 87

690- Full inservice all 6, 7, 8 grade teachers/all schools
691- Design ongoing staff development for all new teachers in middle school
990- Board Report X

*Numbers in left column indicate a category of events and the order of change (i.e., 800 = evaluation, 22 = audit number 22.)

Figure 26. Calendar of Events

	Summer 84 0-9	Fall 84 10-19	Spring 85 20-29	Summer 85 30-39	Fall 85 40-49
Facilities & Special Programs Placement (100-199)	100			130	140
Curriculum (200-299)	200 201 202	210 211 212	220 221 222 223 224	230	240
Administrator/Supervisor Training (300-399)		310	320	330 331	340
Public Relations (400-499)			420		440
Transportation & Redistricting (500-599)				530	
Teacher Training (600-699)			620 621 622		640
Instructional Materials (700-799)					740 741
Evaluation (800-899)	800 801	810 811 812	820 821 822		840
Board Reports (900-999)	900	910	920	930	940

| | Spring 86
50-59 | Summer 86
60-69 | Fall 86
70-79 | Spring 87
80-89 | Summer 87
90-99 |
|---|---|---|---|---|---|
| Facilities & Special Programs Placement
(100-199) | | | | | |
| Curriculum
(200-299) | | | 270 | | |
| Administrator/Supervisor Training
(300-399) | | 360 | | | |
| Public Relations
(400-499) | 450 | | 470 | 480 | |
| Transportation & Redistricting
(500-599) | | | | | |
| Teacher Training
(600-699) | | 660
661 | | 680 | 690
691 |
| Instructional Materials
(700-799) | | | 770 | | |
| Evaluation
(800-899) | | | 870 | | |
| Board Reports
(900-999) | 950 | 960 | 970 | 980 | 990 |

Figure 27. Outline of Progress Reports for Middle Schools in Orange County

In September 1983 the Orange County School Board committed the district to a new intermediate grade pattern (grades 6-8) based on the middle school concept. It was determined that by fall of 1987, Orange County would have the middle school organization in all of its 19 intermediate schools. Since that time, three progress reports on the transition process have been presented to the board, with a fourth report being presented at this time.

PROGRESS REPORT #1 outlined the rationale for the transition to the middle school concept, as well as a suggested approach to the conversion process. The report also listed the committees to be used throughout the process and also a review of data collected in surveys of students, parents, teachers, and administrators.

PROGRESS REPORT #2 presented the proposed Orange County Middle School Design, emphasizing a balanced program of subject content, personal development, and essential skills. Also found in this report were a suggested middle school staffing pattern, an organizational plan, and possible facilities considerations.

PROGRESS REPORT #3 outlined the steps used in developing a curriculum appropriate for middle-level students. It also included a preliminary report from the staff development and public relations committees. Finally, this report presented a sample of the curriculum developed by each of the 36 ad hoc committees.

PROGRESS REPORT #4 presents an overall evaluation of progress since the fall of 1983 and also projections for completion of our reorganization to the middle school concept. It should be noted that as we move closer to our target date of August 1987, the evaluation committee will have a greater role in the process. This is to guarantee that Orange County can, with confidence, say "COMING SOON, AMERICA'S BEST MIDDLE SCHOOLS."

Figure 28. A Comprehensive Plan for Middle Schools Schedule of Events 1985-86

Scheduled Event	Time	Person Responsible
Final Revision—Printing of Curriculum Maps	Summer 1985	Program Consultants
Coordination of Subject Areas—Selection of Interdisciplinary Concepts	Summer 1985	Program Consultants
Field Testing of Mapped Curriculums	1985-86 1986-87	Program Consultants
Identification of Training Needs in Program-Subject Areas—Short and Long-Range (to Staff Development Committee)	Summer 1985	Program Consultants
Development—Monitoring of Quality Indicators	1985-88	Management Team
Career Counseling—Identification of Future Leadership	Summer 1985	
Staff Development Plan Completed	Fall 1985	Staff Development Committee

Scheduled Event	Time	Person Responsible
Training Program for Future Leadership—Continuing Administrative-Prospective Administrative Coordinators	Fall 1985 Spring 1986	Staff Development Committee
Certification Training—Inservice for all Prospective Middle School Personnel	Fall 1985 Summer 1987	Staff Development Committee
Survey and Teacher Preference	Fall 1986	
Sustaining Inservice for all Middle School Personnel	Fall 1987	
Administrative Staffing Pattern Design, Schedule Finalized	June 1986	Management Team
Budget Recommendations for Middle School Conversion for 1986-87	Feb 1986	
Budget Recommendations for Middle School Conversion for 1987-88	Feb 1986	
Facilities Modification 1985-87	Fall 1985	Management Team
School Size—Redistricting—Staffing Patterns—Transportation—Transfer of Books, Materials—Job Descriptions for all Middle School Personnel	Fall 1986	Management Team
Final Placement of Teachers—Administrators—Others for 1987-88 Opening	Spring 1987	Management Team
Articulation–Elementary–Middle–High School	Fall 1986	Management Team
Development of New Reporting—Grading System for Middle School	Spring 1986	Management Team
Evaluation of Process/Products of Middle School Conversion	1984-88	Evaluation Committee
School-Based Improvement Plans Developed—Pilot Programs Implemented	Fall 1985 Spring 1987	Middle School Principals—Directors
Monitoring of School-Based Improvement Plans	Fall 1985 Spring 1987	Directors
Public Relations Program For Conversion—(Plan to Management Team—Fall 1985)	Fall 1985 Spring 1987	
Management Team Meetings	Sept-Oct-Dec Feb-April-May 1985-88	Management Team
Board Reports	Dec-June 1985-88	Management Team
Coordinating Committee Meetings	Sept-Nov-Feb April 1985-87	Management Team
Leadership Seminars/Planning for Principals and Assistants	Oct-Nov-Feb April-Summer 1985-86	Management Team
Planned Problem Resolution/Organization of Sustaining Orange County League of Middle Schools	Oct-Nov-Dec Feb-March- May 1987-88	Middle School Principals

Figure 29. Middle School Semester Transition Schedule

Date	Activity
August 28	Middle school management team meeting
September 5	Initial board report to board secretary
September 11	Middle school status report to school board
September 13, 9:00-11:00 a.m.	Meeting with state department personnel regarding research grants
September 13, 1:00-4:00 p.m.	Coordinating committee—orientation meeting
October 2, a.m.	Evaluation committee first meeting
October 2, p.m.	Coordinating committee (second meeting) • Establish subcommittees • Form design committee • Perform tasks assigned
October 16, a.m.	Junior high principals receive school profiles
October 16, a.m.	Middle school management team meeting
October 16, p.m.	Design committee orientation • Set standards for Orange County middle schools
October 30	Design committee workday
October 30, p.m.	Building level assessments sent out
November 8	Design committee report completed
November 13	Coordinating committee (third meeting) receives design committee report and work on curriculum management plan
November 20, a.m.	Middle school management team meeting
November 20, p.m.	Workday
November 27	Writing workday—middle school management plan
December 4	Coordinating committee • Curriculum Management Plan Report finalized • Appoint Staff Development Committee • Appoint Program Development Committee
December 11	Middle school report to school board • Standards • Curriculum Management Plan • Preliminary Evaluation
December 18	Middle school management team planning for January-June

Figure 30. Sample Middle School Committee Calendar

Committee	Date	Time	Location
Business Education	2/01/85	8:00 a.m.-4:30 p.m.	Personnel Conf. Rm.
Extra Curricular	2/04/85	1:00 p.m.	Board Room
Program Development	2/05/85	8:30 a.m.-3:30 p.m.	Mid Florida Tech
Career Ed.	2/08/85	8:00 a.m.-3:30 p.m.	Delaney Auditorium
Foreign Language	2/13/85	8:30 a.m.	Woods Inservice CR
Computer	2/15/85	8:00 a.m.	Audubon Park Elem.
Alt. Ed. ad hoc	2/18/85	8:30 a.m.	Delaney
Reading	2/19/85	9:00 a.m.	Vocational Conf. Rm.
Extra-curricular	2/19/95	7:00 p.m.	Westridge Jr. High
Art	2/20/85	9:00 a.m.	Board Rm. Conf. B
Music	2/20/85	8:00 a.m.	Personnel Conf. Rm.
Student Services	2/20/85	9:00 a.m.-2:00 p.m.	Delaney
Extra-curricular	2/20/85	7:00 p.m.	West Orange High
Computer	2/22/85	8:00 a.m.	Audubon Park Elem.
Physical Education	2/22/85	8:00 a.m.-3:00 p.m.	Board Rm. Conf. B
Career ad hoc	2/22/85	8:00 a.m.-3:30 p.m.	Delaney Auditorium
Library Media	2/22/85	8:30 a.m.-12:00 noon	Board Rm. Conf. Rm. A
Extra Curricular	2/26/85	7:00 p.m.	Glenridge Jr. High
Extra-Curricular	2/27/85	7:00 p.m.	Carver Jr. High
Alternative Ed.	2/28/85	8:30 a.m.	Delaney
Industrial Arts	2/28/85	8:00 a.m.-3:00 p.m.	Personnel Conf. Rm.
Computer ad hoc	3/01/85	8:00 a.m.	Audubon Park Elem.
Business Education	3/01/85	8:00 a.m.-4:30 p.m.	Personnel Conf. Rm.
Home Economics	3/01/85	12:30 p.m.-3:30 p.m.	Upstairs Conf. Rm.

Figure 31. Scheduled Events for Middle School Planning Accomplishments to Date

Scheduled Event	Projected Date	Person Responsible	Accomplishment	Date Accomplished
Final revision and printing of curriculum maps	08/85	Program Consultants	Curriculum reviewed by Program Development Committee	04/85
			Revision by writing team	04/85
			Second review by Program Development Committee	05/85
			Presented to Coordinating Committee	05/17/85
			Presented to School Board, Progress Report 3	06/11/85
			Final printing	09/85
			Two copies of Proposed Middle School Curriculum for each program distributed to junior high schools and one copy to elementary and secondary program consultants	10/85
Coordination of subject areas, selection of interdisciplinary concepts	08/85	Program Consultants	Writing teams produced *Tying It All Together*, a handbook on the development of interdisciplinary units, and *Test Taking Skills*, *Problem Solving Skills*, and *Listening Skills*, which are a compilation of activities to address skills identified as essential for middle school	Summer 1985
Field-testing of mapped curricula	1985-86 1986-87	Program Consultants	Curriculum field-testing was begun during second nine weeks	11/85
Identification of training needs in programs and subject areas, short and long-range, to Staff Development Committee	08/85	Program Consultants	Target groups to receive instruction were identified, including administrators, instructional staff, and classified personnel	06/85
Development and monitoring of quality indicators	1985-88	Management Team	Standards for Achievement of OCPS Middle School Design are being used by principals for self-diagnosis	09/85
Career counseling, identification of future leadership	08/85		One person per junior high school identified for training	09/85

Task	Date	Responsible	Description	Timeline
Staff development plan completed	11/85	Staff Development Committee	See Staff Development Committee report for identified target groups, description of training, and timeline for training. Different training component needs (levels of awareness and information) were identified for the different groups. In addition to the OCPS component, UCF is also developing a middle school certification program, which will provide resources to the district and provide an alternative method of certification.	06/85
Training program for future leadership: continuing and prospective administrators and program consultants	10/85-08/86	Staff Development Committee	Five training sessions conducted for principals. Five training sessions conducted for API's and program consultants. Leadership seminars (9 sessions) conducted for selected school-based instructional personnel representing each junior high school.	02/85-05/85 09/27-12/13/85 09/85-12/85
Certification training, inservice for all prospective middle school personnel	10/85-08/87	Staff Development Committee	The district's middle school certification component provided in ten Thursday night sessions to 55 teachers on a voluntary basis; training incorporates topics contained in PRIME legislation.	09/85-11/85
Survey of teacher preference	09/85		See Teacher Preference Survey and analysis.	09/85
Sustaining inservice for all middle school personnel	10/87		Inservice for junior high principals, identified potential leaders, API's, program consultants, and 55 teachers as outlined above.	09/85-12/85
Facilities modification for 1985-87	11/85	Management Team	Facilities review begun to enhance match between current and desired middle school plant; modifications included in District Capital Outlay Plan.	09/85
Evaluation of process/products of middle school conversion	1984-88	Evaluation Committee	Stages of Concern Questionnaire and Open-Ended Statement of Concern administered to junior high administrators and teachers; results presented at Junior High League meeting in June and to all junior high principals, API's, and secondary program consultants in September. Profiles provided for each junior high school to show data on enrollment, teacher and student attendance, discipline, and achievements.	05/85-09/85 09/85

Figure 31. Scheduled Events for Middle School Planning Accomplishments to Date

Scheduled Event	Projected Date	Person Responsible	Accomplishment	Date Accomplished
School-based improvement plans developed; pilot programs implemented	11/85-04/87	Middle School Principals and Directors	School-based improvement plans based on the Middle School Design shared among junior high principals; these included areas of curriculum, staff/instructional, facilities, and organizational changes. Pilot programs being implemented during second nine-weeks.	09/85 11/85
Monitoring of school-based improvement plans	11/85-04/87	Directors	Standards for Achievement of Middle School Design will be utilized.	
Public relations program for conversion (plan submitted to Management Team—Fall, 1985)	11/85-04/87		See Middle School Communication Plan and Middle School: The Right Connection (brochure), which were developed by the Community Relations Department and the Middle School Public Relations Committee.	09/85
Management Team meetings	Sept-Oct-Dec-Feb-Apr-May, 1985-88	Management Team	Three management team meetings	09/85, 10/85, 11/85
Board Reports	Dec/June 1985-88	Management Team	Four progress reports have been submitted.	12/85
Coordinating Committee meetings	Sept-Oct-Nov-Feb-April 1985-87	Management Team	Curriculum presented. October agenda included evaluation report, standards of achievement, products from public relations, Teacher Preference Survey, and enhancement grant interim report. Two ad hoc committees appointed: articulation and student-grade reporting.	05/85 10/85
Planned problem resolution	Oct-Nov-Dec-Feb-Mar-May, 1987-88	Middle School Principals	Middle School agenda items are discussed at monthly junior high principals meetings.	09/85, 10/85, 11/85

Figure 32. Middle School Communication Plan

MISSION

To effectively communicate the advantages of the middle school concept while bolstering acceptance and support for the program.

GOALS

1. To communicate the advantages of the reorganized system to the targeted publics.
2. To gain acceptance of the middle school concept by parents and community groups.
3. To promote acceptance and goodwill for the program among students, teachers and administrators.
4. To create name awareness, visibility, and credibility for the program within the district and the United States.

Figure 33. Middle School Communication Plan Activities and Timeline September 1985 through September 1987

Activities	Audience	Responsibility	Timeline	Status
1. Write and distribute articles and press releases to principals, student newspapers, PTA/LSAC chairmen, Ministerial Association members, city government and business/professional organizations for use in their newsletters.	Staff, parents and community	Community Relations Department	As needed	Ongoing
2. Design a brochure outlining the goals and philosophy of the middle school.	Parents and community	Community Relations Department	By Sept. 1985	Completed
3. Establish a slogan and logo for use with all middle school materials.	Staff, parents and community	Middle School PR Committee	By July 1985	Completed
4. Establish a regular middle school column in the *Educator*.	Staff and community	Community Relations Department	Begin Sept. 1985	Ongoing
5. Write and distribute press releases to local media.	Staff and community	Community Relations Department	As needed	Ongoing
6. Coordinate appearances on various radio and TV talk shows.	Staff and community	Intermediate Education Department	As needed until Sept. 1986. Regularly thereafter.	Ongoing
7. Use restaurant tray liners to develop an awareness of the middle school move.	Community	Middle School PR Committee	Spring–Summer 1987	
8. Use advertising space on school milk cartons to develop an awareness of the move to middle schools in 1987.	Students	Middle School PR Committee	During 1986-87 school year	
9. Expand the Middle School Speakers Bureau to provide more presentations to staff members, parent and civic groups, and student councils.	Staff, parents and community	Intermediate Education Department	Select and train speakers beginning Sept. 1985. As needed thereafter.	Ongoing

10. Make videotape copies of the middle school slide-tape presentation and encourage their use at various staff and parent meetings.	Staff and parents	Intermediate Education Department	By Sept. 1985. Promote in publications.	Completed Ongoing
11. Provide regular middle school updates in the *Orange Peal*.	Staff members	Community Relations Department	Beginning Sept. 1985	Ongoing
12. Provide regular middle school updates in *Teamwork*.	Staff members	Intermediate Education Department	Beginning Sept. 1985	Ongoing
13. Establish a middle school hotline number that staff and community members can call for accurate, up-to-the-minute information.	Staff, parents and community	Intermediate Education Department	By Sept. 1985	Completed
14. Work with the Classroom Teachers Association to include middle school updates in their regular publications.	Staff members		Beginning Sept. 1985	Ongoing
15. Design distinctive middle school stationery for use with all press releases.	Staff and media	Middle School PR Committee	By Jan. 1986	
16. Work with TV and/or radio stations to produce documentaries on the middle schools.	Staff and community	Community Relations Department	Spring—Summer 1987	
17. Provide a news media orientation session.	News media	Community Relations Department	Sept. 1986	
18. Develop book covers, T-shirts, stickers and other items to promote the middle school transition.	Students, staff and community	Middle School PR Committee	Spring 1986	

References

Association for Supervision and Curriculum Development. "Profile of a Middle School." Videotape. Alexandria, Va.: ASCD, 1976.

Bennett, William J. *What Works—Research About Teaching and Learning*. Washington, D.C.: U.S. Department of Education, 1986.

Elkind, David. *All Grown Up and No Place To Go: Teenagers in Crisis*. Reading, Mass.: Addison Wesley Publisher, 1984.

National Association of Secondary School Principals. *An Agenda for Excellence at the Middle Level*. Reston, Va.: NASSP, 1986.

Wiles, Jon, and Joseph Bondi. *A Guide and Plan for Conducting Ten Workshops with the NEA Middle School Training Program*. Washington, D.C.: National Education Association, 1985.

Wiles, Jon, and Joseph Bondi. *The Essential Middle School*. Tampa, Fla.: Wiles, Bondi, and Associates, 1986a.

Wiles, Jon, and Joseph Bondi. *The Middle School We Need*. Alexandria, Va.: ASCD, revised 1986b.

Appendix A

Sample Survey Instruments & Forms

MIDDLE SCHOOL (GRADES 6-8) OPINIONNAIRE, PARENT FORM

Please rate each of the following ideas about middle schools *to show how important each one is to you and your child*. Choose the answer that you feel is best and place the corresponding number in the blank space. Use the key below to show your feelings.

1	2	3	4	5
Very Important	Important	Fairly Important	Not Very Important	Not Important At All

EXAMPLE: If having guidance and counseling service available for each student is "Fairly Important" to you, you would place a "3" in the blank space.

_____ 1. Guidance and counseling services should be available for each student.

_____ 2. Each student should have at least one teacher who knows him/her well.

_____ 3. Small group and individual guidance should also be provided by a classroom teacher under the direction of the school counselor.

_____ 4. Opportunities for after-school social activities (such as dances, athletic games, boosters) should be provided for students.

_____ 5. Opportunities should be provided to help students develop good attitudes and standards for themselves.

_____ 6. Club activities should be scheduled during the day to provide opportunities for group work in areas of common interest.

_____ 7. Students should expand and discover their individual interests and aptitudes through exploratory and enrichment courses (such as home economics, band, creative writing).

_____ 8. Remedial instruction should be available to assist students who have difficulty in mastering basic skills.

_____ 9. A wide variety of intramural activities (team competition within the same school) should be offered to allow all students to participate.

_____ 10. Physical education should emphasize health, physical fitness, and lifetime sports.

_____ 11. Students should have an opportunity to express creativity through student newspapers, drama, and music.

_____ 12. A variety of teaching methods and materials should be utilized rather than a single textbook approach.

_____ 13. Students should use and apply basic skills through projects and "hands-on" activities.

_____ 14. Students should proceed at their own rate according to their abilities.

_____ 15. Behavior problems should be handled, when possible, by teachers and parents without the involvement of the administrators.

_____ 16. Major disciplinary problems should be handled by the school administrators.

_____ 17. An alternative program to suspension should be provided for students having behavior problems (in-school suspension program).

_____ 18. Opportunities should be provided for parents to have a conference with all of their child's teachers at the same time.

Appendix A

MIDDLE SCHOOL ANALYSIS SURVEY

This survey is part of a review of the status of middle school programs in Orange County. Principals, with the assistance of a counselor and at least one other staff member, are requested to complete the following analysis survey. Responses should represent a consensus among the committee. Check either yes or no to the following questions about *your* school. Please give careful thought to analyzing each question carefully. Qualifying comments may be added in the space provided at the conclusion of the survey.

Name of School _____

Survey Committee: Principal _____

Guidance Counselor _____

Other Staff Member _____
(Name and Position)

YES   NO   PHILOSOPHY AND GOALS

___ ___   1. A formal *middle school-oriented* philosophy exists and is accepted by the faculty.

___ ___   2. The goals of the school program reflect a three-part thrust: a) personal development, b) skills for continued learning, and c) education for social competence.

___ ___   3. The philosophy and goals of this school were formulated following a complete assessment of the needs of students attending the school.

ORGANIZATION/ADMINISTRATION

___ ___   4. The school utilizes a "house plan" or "school-within-school" arrangement.

___ ___   5. The school day is flexibly scheduled using large blocks of time and "modular" time arrangements.

___ ___   6. Teachers are organized into interdisciplinary planning/teaching teams that share a common group of students and planning period.

___ ___   7. Teaching teams are located in physical proximity to one another.

___ ___   8. Parent involvement/community involvement is "built-in" to the school curriculum.

CURRICULUM/ORGANIZED LEARNING

9. The formal program of organized learning includes the following components:

___ ___   A. Core academic learning consisting of language arts, mathematics, social studies, science

___ ___   B. Remedial and enrichment opportunities such as gifted programs

YES	NO	
—	—	C. Exploring electives to expose new fields of knowledge and expand aesthetic and creative horizons
—	—	D. Career education components for all students
—	—	E. Physical development and health education for all students
—	—	F. Student-initiated elective choices in art, music, and other related areas
—	—	G. A required course in the area of computer literacy

10. General skill development is planned and included in major subject areas including:

—	—	A. Reading
—	—	B. Spelling
—	—	C. Writing/Penmanship
—	—	D. Library use skills
—	—	E. Problem solving
—	—	F. Finding and organizing information
—	—	G. Critical and creative thinking

11. A continuous progress approach to learning is present which does the following:

—	—	A. Assesses each student at entry level on a continuum of course objectives
—	—	B. Has ongoing monitoring to determine each student's readiness to progress in curriculum
—	—	C. Allows student to attain proficiency in skills and performance objectives at rate/level that matches the student's instructional needs
—	—	D. Assesses student performance based on progress through a skill-and-objective continuum

12. A schoolwide advisement program is present which consists of the following:

—	—	A. Includes a separate, planned nonacademic program
—	—	B. Is directed by guidance counselors
—	—	C. Is a regularly scheduled group activity
—	—	D. Involves all certificated personnel, staff, and support personnel
—	—	E. Provides ongoing personal interaction between staff (advisor) and students (advisee)
—	—	F. Maintains a teacher/pupil ratio of less than 1:20
—	—	G. Provides individual guidance opportunities when needed

13. A physical development/health program is present and consists of the following:

—	—	A. Experienced by all students
—	—	B. Students grouped on basis of development rather than grade level

APPENDIX A

      C. Intramural program available to all students and organized around skill development

      D. Formal health program to assist students in understanding and accepting physical and intellectual changes in themselves and others

      E. Provides health screening and monitoring for all students

      F. Provides graduated physical education program according to student development

INSTRUCTIONAL PATTERNS

14. Students are grouped by intellectual, social, and/or physical characteristics in classes

15. A variety of instructional methods is found in classes at any given time in the school day.

16. Instructional strategies other than lecture are found in most classrooms.

17. Varied instructional materials (multilevel texts, teacher-made materials) are regularly used in classes.

18. There is an interdisciplinary team planning/teaching approach that provides for the following:

      A. Teachers of different subjects meet during scheduled time to coordinate instruction for common group of students.

      B. Teachers of different subjects meet during scheduled time to monitor progress of common group of students.

      C. Teachers of different subjects teach common group of students within block of time and group/regroup students to meet varied instructional objectives.

      D. Teachers of different subjects participate in delivery of interdisciplinary units on periodic basis.

      E. Teachers of different subjects meet together with parents of individual students to discuss the student's program.

As necessary, give qualifying comments about specific questions or items within questions. Please indicate the specific question being addressed; e.g., 13 C.

MIDDLE SCHOOL OPINONNAIRE, ADMINISTRATOR AND TEACHER FORM

(To be completed by all administrators and all 7th and 8th grade teachers and counselors.)

A separate computer General Purpose Answer Sheet is provided to record your answers. On the left portion of Side 1, please bubble only these columns:

Special Codes, Columns K-N   School Number

Special Codes, Column O   Teachers bubble a 1
                                 Counselors bubble a 2
                                 Administrators bubble a 3

Please rate each of the following ideas about middle schools *to show how important each one is to you*. Choose the answer that you feel is best and blacken the bubble with the number of that choice on the separate computer General Purpose Answer Sheet. *Use a Number 2 pencil only*. Use the key below to show your feelings.

1	2	3	4	5
Very Important	Important	Fairly Important	Not Very Important	Not Important At All

EXAMPLE: If having guidance and counseling service available for each student is "Fairly Important" to you, you would place a "3" in the blank space.

1. Guidance and counseling services should be available for each student.

2. Each student should have at least one teacher who knows him/her well.

3. Small-group and individual guidance should also be provided by a classroom teacher under the direction of the school counselor.

4. Opportunities for after-school social activities (such as dances, athletic games, boosters) should be provided for students.

5. Opportunities should be provided to help students develop good attitudes and standards for themselves.

6. Club activities should be scheduled during the day to provide opportunities for group work in areas of common interest.

7. Students should expand and discover their individual interests and aptitudes through exploratory and enrichment courses (such as home economics, band, creative writing).

8. Remedial instruction should be available to assist students who have difficulty in mastering basic skills.

9. A wide variety of intramural activities (team competition within the same school) should be offered to allow all students to participate.

10. Physical education should emphasize health, physical fitness, and lifetime sports.

APPENDIX A

11. Students should have an opportunity to express creativity through student newspapers, drama, and music.

12. A variety of teaching methods and materials should be utilized rather than a single textbook approach.

13. Students should use and apply basic skills through projects and "hands-on" activities.

14. Students should proceed at their own rate according to their abilities.

15. Behavior problems should be handled, when possible, by teachers and parents without the involvement of the administrators.

16. Major disciplinary problems should be handled by the school administrators.

17. An alternative program to suspension should be provided for students having behavior problems (in-school suspension program).

18. Opportunities should be provided for parents to have a conference with all of their child's teachers at the same time.

19. Parent volunteers should be involved assisting in the classroom.

20. Sixth grade students should receive special attention as they make the transition to the middle school (for example, orientation programs, individual and group guidance services).

21. Course development should reflect a coordinated curriculum.

22. A well-defined district scope and sequence should be available for each academic discipline.

23. Instruction should be planned and delivered based upon formal and informal assessment of student skills.

24. Schoolwide opportunities should be provided to help students develop good attitudes and standards for themselves.

25. A team of teachers should plan and implement the basic instructional program for a given group of students, i.e., an English, math, social studies, science, and reading teacher working with the same students.

26. Physical and health education programs should emphasize understanding and care of the body at this stage of development.

27. The middle school program should be a unique program bridging the gap between the elementary schools and the secondary schools.

28. Provisions should be made for short-term exploration/enrichment activities in addition to the regularly scheduled electives.

29. A common planning period should be provided for teams of teachers who work with the same students.

30. Opportunities should be provided for students to understand the community in which they live and to develop an attitude for community improvement.

MIDDLE SCHOOL CHARACTERISTICS

(To be completed by all administrators and all seventh and eighth grade teachers and counselors.)

This is a continuation of data collection after you have completed the Middle School Opinionnaire. Note that the items begin with Number 31. Be sure to bubble beside the appropriate number.

Rate each of the following characteristics in terms of importance by blackening the appropriate bubble, 1-5, on the answer sheet. Use the same key as for the Middle School Opinionnaire, with a "1" indicating "Very Important" and a "5" indicating "Not Important At All."

CHARACTERISTICS

31. **Guidance Services:** Both group and individual guidance services should be available. The guidance program should be a total school concern and both teachers and professional counselors must be involved.

32. **Home-based teachers (or security factor):** Each student should have at least one teacher who knows him/her personally. Meetings with that teacher should be on a daily basis.

33. **Social Experience:** The sophisticated social activities that emulate high school programs should not be included; e.g., early dating, night dances, competitive interscholastic athletics.

34. **Personal Values and Standards:** The program should provide opportunities for helping children to formulate personal values and standards.

35. **Gradual Transition:** Experiences should be provided that assist early adolescents in making the adjustment from dependence to gradual independence through a program that articulates well with the elementary and high schools.

36. **Exploratory and Enrichment Studies:** The program should provide opportunities for children to explore their individual interests via a combination of required and elective courses.

37. **Basic Skill Repair and Extension:** The program should provide opportunities for students to receive clinical help in learning basic skills, including skills of continued learning.

38. **Creative Experiences:** The program should include opportunities for students to express themselves creatively. Student-centered, student-directed, student-developed activities should be encouraged; e.g., student newspapers, dramatic creations.

39. **Physical and Health Education:** These activities should be based solely on the needs of the students. Participation rather than spectatorship should be encouraged in a wide variety of intramural activities. A strong health program must be included to help students understand, care for, and use their bodies

40. **Community Relations:** Programs should be provided for students to understand the community and to develop an attitude for community improvement. Community resources should be utilized and the school facilities used by community groups.

Appendix A

41. **Continuing Progress:** The program should feature a nongraded organization that would allow students to progress at their own rate.

42. **Multimaterial Approach:** The program should be planned to involve the use of a variety of easily accessible learning materials rather than a basic textbook approach.

43. **Flexible Schedules:** This is to allow for the use of block time for basic subjects/exploratory or special interest classes, as the need arises.

44. **Individualized/Personalized Instruction:** This approach goes hand in hand with continuous progress and considers the varying intellectual growth rates of the students.

45. **Team Teaching:** The program should allow students to interact with a variety of teachers in a wide range of subject areas. Interdisciplinary team teaching is encouraged.

46. **Evaluation:** Evaluation of the student's work should be positive, nonthreatening, and individualized. Student self-evaluation should be encouraged.

47. **Student Services:** Students should be made aware of the broad spectrum of specialized services available to them. The program should provide for the broadest possible range of specialists available via government and other agencies.

48. **Diversity in Teacher Certification:** The middle school staff should include teachers certified as elementary and teachers certified as secondary.

49. **Auxiliary Staffing:** The middle school should utilize personnel such a volunteer parents, teacher aides, clerical aides, and other support staff.

HOW I FEEL ABOUT MYSELF
STUDENT FORM B

(To be completed by a sample of students in seventh and eighth grade.)

We would like to find out how seventh and eighth grade students feel about themselves. Below is a list of statements that apply to middle school students. There are no right or wrong answers. A separate computer General Purpose Answer Sheet is provided to record your answers. On the left portion of side 1, please bubble only as follows:

Grade	Your current grade
Identification Number, Column A	Bubble a 2
Special Codes, Columns K-N	School number

Read the statement and mark whether you think it is *"like you"* or *"not like you."* Using the key below, blacken the bubble below the letter of that choice on the separate computer answer sheet. *Use a Number 2 pencil only.*

> A. Like me
> B. Not like me

1. I spend a lot of time daydreaming.
2. I'm pretty sure of myself.
3. I often wish I were someone else.
4. I'm easy to like.
5. I never worry about anything.
6. I find it very hard to talk in front of the class.
7. I wish I were younger.
8. There are lots of things about myself I'd change if I could.
9. I can make up my mind without too much trouble.
10. I'm a lot of fun to be with.
11. I get upset easily.
12. I always do the right thing.
13. I'm proud of my schoolwork.
14. Someone always has to tell me what to do.
15. It takes me a long time to get used to anything new.

Appendix A

16. I'm often sorry for the things I do.
17. I'm popular with kids my own age.
18. Adults usually consider my feelings.
19. I'm never unhappy.
20. I'm doing the best work that I can.
21. I give in very easily.
22. I can usually take care of myself.
23. I'm pretty happy.
24. I would rather play with children younger than me.
25. Adults expect too much of me.
26. I like everyone I know.
27. I like to be called on in class.
28. I understand myself.
29. It's pretty tough to be me.
30. Things are all mixed up in my life.
31. Kids usually follow my ideas.
32. No one pays much attention to me.
33. I never get scolded.
34. I'm not doing as well in school as I'd like to.
35. I can make up my mind and stick to it.
36. I really don't like being who I am.
37. I have a low opinion of myself.
38. I don't like to be with other people.
39. There are many times when I'd like to run away.
40. I'm never shy.
41. I often feel upset in school.
42. I often feel ashamed of myself.
43. I'm not as nice looking as most people.
44. If I have something to say, I usually say it.

45. Kids pick on me very often.
46. I always tell the truth.
47. My teacher makes me feel I'm not good enough.
48. I don't care what happens to me.
49. I'm a failure.
50. I get upset easily when I'm scolded.
51. Most people are better liked than I am.
52. I usually feel as if adults are pushing me.
53. I always know what to say to people.
54. I often get discouraged in school.
55. Things usually don't bother me.
56. I can't be depended on.
57. I can usually get passing grades without working too hard.
58. I think the things I do in school are going to help me be successful when I grow up.
59. School is hard work for me.
60. Things that happen outside of school often worry me at school.

STUDENT VALUE SURVEY

The directions for this section are different from the usual. Teachers and students please work together to be sure responses are recorded correctly. Choose from the list below the five that are of the most importance in your life. For each of your five choices, bubble a "1" next to the appropriate number on the answer sheet. NOTE: For items 61-71, you will bubble *only* for five items. The others should be left blank.

61. A COMFORTABLE LIFE (nice house, plenty of money)
62. EQUALITY (brotherhood; equal chance for all, rich or poor, black or white, man or woman)
63. FAMILY SECURITY (family getting along together, all living together, all caring for each other)
64. SELF-RESPECT (liking yourself, feeling good about what you do)
65. SENSE OF ACCOMPLISHMENT (doing something worthwhile for society; making a lasting contribution)
66. FREEDOM (being independent, having free choice)

APPENDIX A

67. HAPPINESS (personal contentment)
68. TRUE FRIENDSHIP (having friends who are close and loyal)
69. EXCITING LIFE (fun-filled, active, enjoyable)
70. WORLD AT PEACE (no wars, riots, less crime and violence)
71. GOOD EDUCATION (opportunity to finish high school, go on to college or further training)

INSTRUCTION PREFERENCE INDICATOR
STUDENT FORM A

(To be completed by a sample of students in seventh and eighth grade.)

We would like to find out how seventh and eighth grade students feel about some things. There are no right or wrong answers. A separate computer General Purpose Answer Sheet is provided to record your answers. On the left portion of side 1, please bubble only these columns:

Grade	Your current grade
Identification Number, Column A	Bubble a 1
Special Codes, Columns K-N	School Number

Below is a list of learning activities that you might be asked to participate in at school. Choose the answer for each activity that tells *how helpful you feel each activity is* and blacken the bubble with the number of that choice on the computer answer sheet. *Use a Number 2 pencil only.* Please use the following key to show how you feel.

1	2	3
Very Helpful	Fairly Helpful	Not Helpful At All

1. Having other students present reports to the class

2. Going to the library with a committee to look up information

3. Having a friend help you learn material you are finding difficult

4. Studying on your own to learn new information

5. Discussing class material with a small group of other students

6. Having the teacher ask the class questions about material that was assigned to be studied or read

7. Listening to the ideas of other students during class discussion of some topic

8. Working with other students on a project the teacher suggests

9. Working on assignments on a ditto sheet

10. Discussing an issue when your opinion is different from that of another student

11. Learning about a topic such as an historical event, a job interview, or an election campaign by acting it out in class

12. Having the teacher give specific instructions about how to do things

13. Doing assignments where you can find out immediately whether your answers are correct

14. Sharing ideas of your own with other students during class discussion of some topic

15. Hearing a guest speaker talk about a subject you are studying in class

16. Doing research in the library for a paper you are assigned to write
17. Having a student in your class work with you to review material for a test
18. Participating in a class drill where the teacher asks for specific information from members of the class
19. Having the teacher explain what is expected of the class on an assignment
20. Taking notes as the teacher talks to the class
21. Working with other students in planning and completing a project
22. Listening as the teacher presents a lesson to the class
23. Working alone on a project you choose yourself
24. Working a whole page of the same kind of problem that you already know how to work
25. Preparing, on your own, a report you will share with your class
26. Being a member of a panel that discusses how to deal with classroom problems
27. Writing a book report about a book you have enjoyed reading
28. Learning about a topic by doing "hands on" or laboratory activities
29. Talking with the teacher about your progress
30. Having classroom activities that help you learn more about yourself

STUDENT OPINIONNAIRE

For items 31-48 there are also no right or wrong answers. Choose the answer that you feel is right for *you,* and blacken the bubble below the letter of that choice on the computer answer sheet.

31. I get along with my teachers and principal.
    - A. Very well
    - B. Pretty well
    - C. Sometimes have trouble
    - D. Often have trouble

32. I think that my school is a nice place to be.
    - A. Very nice place
    - B. Pretty nice place
    - C. Not very nice
    - D. Don't like it

33. My teachers know me as well as I feel they should.
    - A. They know me very well.
    - B. They know me well.
    - C. They know me fairly well.
    - D. They don't know me at all.

34. I feel that I am one of the group in my school.

    A. Yes, I feel that I belong, that I am one of the group.
    B. Mostly yes, though sometimes I am not sure about this.
    C. Mostly no, though sometimes I am not sure about this.
    D. No, I feel that I am not one of the group in my school.

35. My teachers really seem to care about me as a person.

    A. Always   B. Usually   C. Seldom   D. Never

36. In general, I am treated fairly and kindly.

    A. Always   B. Usually   C. Seldom   D. Never

37. I feel safe while I am at my school.

    A. Always   B. Usually   C. Seldom   D. Never

38. What I am studying will be useful to me in everyday living.

    A. Almost everything I study will be useful.
    B. Most of what I study will be useful.
    C. Less than half of what I study will be useful.
    D. Very little of what I study will be useful.

39. I have as much fun at school as I would like to have.

    A. Yes, I have as much fun as I would like to have.
    B. Mostly yes, though sometimes I am not sure.
    C. Mostly no, though sometimes I am not sure.
    D. No, I do not have as much fun as I would like to have.

40. For the most part the teachers in my school are

    A. Always too strict.   B Sometimes too strict.
    C. Never too strict.   D. Not strict enough.

41. My teachers usually give me

    A. All of the help I need with schoolwork.
    B. Most of the help I need with schoolwork.
    C. Some of the help I need with schoolwork.
    D. Very little of the help I need with schoolwork.

42. I feel that the amount of homework I am assigned is

    A. Always the right amount.   B Mostly the right amount.
    C. Too little.   D. Too much.

43. The amount of time I usually spend on homework each school day is

    A. None
    B Between one-half hour and one hour.
    C. Between one and two hours.
    D. More than two hours.

44. I think that I am getting

    A. All that I could get out of my schoolwork.
    B. Somewhat less than I could get out of my schoolwork.
    C. Much less than I could get out of my schoolwork.
    D. Nothing out of my schoolwork.

45. In general, the work my teachers give me is

    A. Not too hard and not too easy — always about right.
    B. Sometimes too hard, other times too easy, but it is usually about right.
    C. Mostly too easy.
    D. Mostly too hard.

JUNIOR HIGH SCHOOL FACILITY SURVEY

Description:

Special Rooms	Exists	Does Not Exist	Needed	Comments
Auditorium				
Gymnasium				
Reading Lab				
Home Economics Room				
Computer Room				
Typing Room				
Art Room				
Choral Room				
Band Room				
Woodwork Shop				
Other Industrial Shops				
Library				
Medical Facility				
Gifted Room				
EH Room				
EMR Room				
SLD Room				
In-School Supervision				
Language Labs				
Unscheduled Rooms				
Health/First Aid Room				
Large Lunch Area				
Team-Teaching Rooms				
Teams				
Adjacent Team Rooms				
Small Rooms for Team Plan'g				
Adjacent Science Labs				
Space for Teaching Aides				
Guidance				
Separate Entry Guidance				
Guidance Secretary				
Private Rooms				
Administration				
Centralized Offices				
Private Discipline Areas				

Appendix A

Description:

Special Rooms	Exists	Does Not Exist	Needed	Comments
Grounds Undeveloped Space Number Major Fields Tennis Courts Basketball Courts Physical Dev. Areas Weight Rooms Dressing Rooms/Showers Courtyards Paved Areas — General Lighted Fields				

Scheduled Renovation Areas:

General Comments About Facility Needs:

MIDDLE SCHOOL TEACHER SURVEY

(To be completed by all seventh and eighth grade teachers and counselors.)

School Name _____

Teacher Name _____
(Please print.)

This questionnaire is designed to gather data from teachers in Orange County about their teaching experience. Place a check in the appropriate blank to indicate your response.

1. Degree(s) held

    ___ A. B.A. or B.S.
    ___ B. B.A. or B.S. plus 15 hours
    ___ C. Master's
    ___ D. Doctorate

2. Total years of teaching experience

    ___ A. One year or less
    ___ B. Two-four years
    ___ C. Five-ten years
    ___ D. 11-19 years
    ___ E. 20 years or more

3. Number of years taught in grades 6, 7, 8

    ___ A. One year or less
    ___ B. Two-four years
    ___ C. Five-ten years
    ___ D. 11-19 years
    ___ E. 20 years or more

4. Certification

    ___ A. Elementary only
    ___ B. Secondary only
    ___ C. K-12
    ___ D. Elementary plus middle school
    ___ E. Secondary plus middle school

Appendix A

5. For the following areas put a check in the blank space if you have current certification in the subject area.

   ___ English

   ___ Math

   ___ Science

   ___ Social Studies

   ___ Reading

   ___ Art

   ___ Music

   ___ Foreign Language

   ___ Physical Education

   ___ Home Economics

   ___ Industrial Arts

   ___ Special Education

   ___ Guidance

   ___ Administration and Supervision

STAFF DEVELOPMENT CHECKLIST FOR MIDDLE SCHOOL TEACHERS

Below you will find 31 skills identified as useful in implementing the middle school concept. From the list, choose the five that you think are most important and necessary for staff development for you and/or your school. Rank them by placing the numbers 1-5 in the appropriate blanks with a "1" indicating the highest priority. For the 31 items, only five items should have a number in the blank space.

_____ 1. Techniques for counseling students

_____ 2. Locating and/or developing appropriate teaching resources

_____ 3. Teaching reading skills in the classroom

_____ 4. Using value-clarification techniques in the classroom

_____ 5. Working with other teachers across subject-matter lines in teams

_____ 6. Planning instructional units

_____ 7. Developing learning centers

_____ 8. Enhancing learner self-concept

_____ 9. Basic classroom management techniques

_____ 10. Record-keeping system in the classroom

_____ 11. Evaluating student progress

_____ 12. Dealing with motivation and discipline problems in the classroom

_____ 13. Teaching for higher thinking and creativity

_____ 14. Promoting effective learning in the classroom

_____ 15. Encouraging learning climates

_____ 16. Individualizing instruction

_____ 17. Grouping and regrouping students for instructional purposes

_____ 18. Developing teacher-made learning materials

_____ 19. Involving students in planning

_____ 20. Understanding culturally diverse students

_____ 21. Using community resources in teaching

_____ 22. Making classrooms more humane

_____ 23. Counseling students one-to-one

Appendix A

_____ 24. Developing interdisciplinary units

_____ 25. Using audiovisuals in teaching

_____ 26. Preparing teacher-made tests

_____ 27. Use of inquiry techniques in teaching

_____ 28. Use of student contracts

_____ 29. Identifying student learning disabilities

_____ 30. Accommodating special education students in the regular classroom

_____ 31. Understanding characteristics of middle school students.

The five most important inservice needs for me or my school are:

1. _____

2. _____

3. _____

4. _____

5. _____

Use the remaining space for any other comments.

TENTH GRADE FOLLOW-UP SURVEY

You have been selected as a sample of 500 tenth graders to provide information on your experience as a junior high school student in Orange County. Please complete the survey and return it in the stamped, self-addressed envelope by May 25, 1984. It is essential that there be a good return rate of the questionnaire to ensure that the results are meaningful. Your assistance in this effort will be greatly appreciated. Your responses will be used to plan for middle school programs (grades 6-8) in the coming years. Please respond to the following items by placing the appropriate number in the blank space. Use the key below to indicate your responses.

1 = Always   2 = Some of the Time   3 = Rarely

Respond to the items based on the way your junior high school showed the following characteristics:

_____ 1. Provided for a gradual transition from the elementary years to the high schools years

_____ 2. Prepared you with the knowledge and learning skills needed for success in the high school

_____ 3. Provided a balanced program that included social as well as academic experiences

_____ 4. Allowed you as an individual to experience frequent and continuous success

_____ 5. Provided teachers who knew you as a person as well as a student

_____ 6. Provided guidance services that met your needs as an individual

_____ 7. Provided a curriculum that was relevant to your needs as a student and individual

_____ 8. Allowed you to explore a wide variety of courses and interests in school

_____ 9. Provided teachers who communicated with one another about the progress of individual students

_____ 10. Provided a type of discipline that fostered independence and the assumption of responsibility

_____ 11. Provided an adequate foundation for academic achievement

_____ 12. Regularly involved your parents in the operation of the school program

_____ 13. Provided ample opportunities for participation in clubs and other social organizations

_____ 14. Provided access to sports and physical development activities of your interest

_____ 15. Provided some caring adult who knew your problems and needs

_____ 16. Provided adequate learning materials to assist you in your studies

_____ 17. Provided a safe and secure environment for education

_____ 18. Provided you with a thorough orientation to the high school curriculum

_____ 19. Provided a fair evaluation of your abilities as a student

_____ 20. Provided an environment (building) that was comfortable and conducive to learning

In the space below, please add additional comments that will help the school district plan for middle schools (grades 6-8).

If you have any questions, please call John Meinicke, program consultant for the intermediate unit, at 422-3200, extension 379.

Appendix B

Characteristics of Emerging Adolescents— Implications For The Middle School

Characteristics of Emerging Adolescents	Implications for the Middle School
Physical Development	
Accelerated physical development begins in transescence marked by increases in weight, height, muscular strength. Boys and girls are growing at varying rates of speed. Girls tend to be taller for the first two years and tend to be more physically advanced. Bone growth is faster than muscle development and the uneven muscle/bone development results in lack of coordination and awkwardness. Bones may lack protection of covering muscles and supporting tendons.	Provide a curriculum that emphasizes self-understanding about body changes. Health and science classes should provide experiences that will develop an understanding about body growth. Guidance counselors and community resource persons such as pediatricians can help students understand what is happening to their bodies. Adaptive physical education classes should be scheduled for students lacking physical coordination. Equipment should be designed for students in transescence to help them develop small and large muscles.
In the pubescent stage for girls, secondary sex characteristics continue to develop with breasts enlarging and menstruation beginning.	Intense sports competition, especially contact sports should be avoided. Schedule sex education classes, health and hygiene seminars for students.

A wide range of individual differences among students begins to appear in pre-pubertal and pubertal stages of development. Although the sequential order of development is relatively consistent in each sex, boys tend to lag a year or two behind girls. There are marked individual differences in physical development for boys and girls. The age of greatest variability in physiological development and physical size is about age 13.

Provide opportunities for interaction among students of multi-ages, but avoid situations where one's physical development can be compared with others (e.g., gang showers).

Intramural programs rather than interscholastic athletics should be emphasized so that each student will have a chance to achieve regardless of physical development. Where interscholastic sports programs exist, the number of games should be limited and games played in the afternoon rather than evening.

Fluctuations in basal metabolism may cause students to be extremely restless at times and listless at others.

The school should provide an opportunity for daily exercise by students and a place where students can be children by playing and being noisy for short periods of time.

Activities such as special interest classes, "hands on" exercises should be encouraged. Students should be allowed to physically move around in their classes and avoid long periods of passive work.

Shows ravenous appetites and peculiar tastes, may overtax the digestive system with large quantities of improper foods.

Snacks should be provided to satisfy between-meal hunger. Guidance should be provided about nutrition as it applies to emerging adolescents.

Social Development

Affiliation base broadens from family to peer group. Conflict sometimes results due to splitting of allegiance between peer group and family.

Teachers should work closely with the family to help adults realize that peer pressure is a normal part of the maturation process. Parents should be encouraged to continue to provide love and comfort to their children even though they may feel their children are rejecting them.

All teachers in the middle school should be counselors. Home-base, teacher-advisor house plan arrangements should be encouraged.

"Puppy love years"—shows extreme devotion to a particular boy or girl friend, but may transfer allegiance to a new friend overnight.

Role playing, guidance exercises can provide students the opportunity to act out feelings. Opportunities should be provided for social interaction between the sexes—parties, games, but not dances in the early grades of the middle school.

Feel the will of the group must prevail—sometimes almost cruel to those not in their group. Copies and displays fads of extremes in clothes, speech, mannerism, and handwriting; very susceptible to advertising.

Set up an active student government so students can develop their own guidelines for dress and behavior. Adults should be encouraged not to react in an outraged manner when extreme dress or mannerisms are displayed by young adolescents.

Strong concern for what is "right" and for social justice. Shows concern for less-fortunate others.	Activities should be planned to allow students to engage in service activities. Peer teaching can be encouraged to allow students to help other students. Community projects such as assisting in a senior citizens club or helping in a child care center can be planned by students and teachers.
Is influenced by adults—attempts to identify with adults other than their parents.	Flexible teaching patterns should prevail so students can interact with a variety of adults with whom they can identify.
Despite a trend toward heterosexual interests, same-sex affiliation tends to dominate during transescence.	Large-group activities rather than boy-girl events should be scheduled. Intramurals can be scheduled so students can interact with friends of the same or opposite sex.
Desire direction and regulation but reserve the right to question or reject suggestions of adults.	The middle school should provide opportunities for students to accept more responsibility in setting standards for behavior. Students should be helped to establish realistic goals and should be assisted in helping realize those goals.

Emotional Development

Is easily offended and sensitive to criticism of personal shortcoming.	Sarcasm by adults should be avoided. Students should be helped to develop values in the solution of their problems.
Students tend to exaggerate simple occurrences and believe their problems are unique.	Socio-drama can be utilized to enable students to see themselves as others see them. Readings dealing with problems similar to their own can help students see that many problems are not unique.

Appendix B

Intellectual Development

Emerging adolescents display a wide range of skills and abilities unique to their developmental patterns.	A variety of approaches and materials in the teaching-learning process should be utilized.
Students range in development from the concrete-manipulatory stage of development to the ability to deal with abstract concepts. The transescent is intensely curious and growing in mental ability.	The middle school should treat students at their own intellectual levels, providing immediate rather than remote goals. All subjects should be individualized. Skill grouping should be flexible.
Middle school learners prefer active over passive learning activities, prefer interaction with peers during learning activities.	Physical movement should be encouraged with small-group discussions, learning centers, and creative dramatics suggested as good activity projects. Provide a program of learning that is exciting and meaningful.
Students in the middle school are usually very curious and exhibit a strong willingness to learn things they consider to be useful. Students enjoy using skills to solve "real life" problems.	Organize curricula around real life concepts such as conflict, competition, peer group influence. Provide activities in both formal and informal situations to improve reasoning powers. Studies of the community, environment are particularly relevant to the age group.

From Jon Wiles and Joseph Bondi, *The Essential Middle School,* 1986a.

Appendix C

Selected Teacher Competencies for Middle School Teachers

1. Possess knowledge of the pre- and early-adolescent physical development which includes knowledge of physical activity needs and the diversity and variety of physical growth rates.

2. Commands knowledge of pre- and early-adolescent intellectual development with emphasis on the transition from concrete to formal levels of mental development.

3. Has a knowledge of a recognized developmental theory and personality theory which can be utilized in identifying appropriate learning strategies for the pre- and early-adolescent.

4. Understands socio-emotional development including the need to adjust to a changing body.

5. Possesses the necessary skills to allow interaction between individual students as well as the opportunity to work in groups of varying sizes.

6. Understands the cultural forces and community relationships that affect the total school curriculum.

7. Has the ability to organize the curriculum to facilitate the developmental tasks of preadolescence and early adolescence.

APPENDIX C

8. Understands the transitional nature of grades 3-6 as they bridge the gap between children of the lower elementary grades and late adolescents and early adults of the upper grades.

9. Possesses the skills needed to work with other teachers and school professionals in team teaching situations.

10. Has the ability to plan multi-disciplinary lessons and/or units and teach them personally or with other professionals.

11. Commands a broad academic background, with specilization in at least two allied areas of the curriculum.

12. Possesses the skill to integrate appropriate media and concrete demonstrations into presentations.

13. Is able to develop and conduct learning situations that will promote independent learning and maximize student choice and responsibility for follow through.

14. Possesses the knowledge and skills that will allow students to sort information, set priorities, and budget time and energy.

15. Is able to teach problem-solving skills and develop lessons that are inquiry oriented.

16. Possesses the ability to recognize difficulties that may be emotional and/or physically based.

17. Possesses the knowledge and skills needed to effectively manage abusive and deviant behavior.

18. Works with extracurricular activities in the school.

19. Gathers appropriate personal information on students using questionnaires, interviews, and observation.

20. Provides frequent feedback to students on learning progress.

21. Functions calmly in a high-activity environment.

22. Handles disruptive behavior in a positive and consistent manner.

23. Builds learning experiences for students based upon learning skills (reading, math) obtained in elementary grades.

24. Works cooperatively with peers, consultants, resource persons and paraprofessionals.

25. Exhibits concern for students by listening and/or empathizing with them.

26. Selects evaluation techniques appropriate to curricular objective in the affective domain.

27. Utilizes value clarification and other affective teaching techniques to help students develop personal value system.

28. Provides an informal, flexible classroom environment.

29. Cooperates in curricular planning and revision.

30. Evaluates the teaching situation and selects the grouping techniques most appropriate for the situation, large-group instruction (100+ students), small-group instruction (15-25 students), or independent study.

31. Uses questioning techniques skillfully to achieve higher-order thinking processes in students.

32. Can move from one type of grouping situation to another smoothly.

33. Functions effectively in various organizational and staffing situations, such as team teaching, differentiated staffing, and multiage groupings.

34. Selects evaluation techniques appropriate to curricular objectives in the psychomotor domain.

35. Establishes positive relationships with the parents and families of students.

36. Works at understanding, accepting and being accepted by members of the subcultures in the school and the community.

*From Jon Wiles and Joseph Bondi, *The Essential Middle School,* Charles Merrill Publishing Company, 1980.

Appendix D

EMERGING ADOLESCENTS — VICTIMS OF A CHANGING SOCIETY

The Most Fragile Group In Our Society

Middle school students have become victims of a changing society. Social problems in our society have had and are having a profound influence on emerging adolescents. Consider the following:

The American Family Is Changing: The "Typical" American Household Does Not Exist Any More

- One of two children will spend some time in a single-parent home by the time they are in the middle grades. Thirty percent of students are latch-key children. Many children spend 3-4 hours at home alone after school before a parent arrives.

- 15 percent of children today are illegitimate.

- Only 16 percent of American households today have the family pattern of a mother at home and a working husband.

- The median age for first marriages for women in 1985 was 23, the highest ever recorded, and 25.5 for men, the highest since 1900. Later marriages and second marriages result in later parenthood. Many parents of middle school students are in their late forties. The number of older mothers tripled in the period between 1970 and 1986.

- More than 40 percent of divorced, separated, or single women received no financial assistance from the fathers of their children.
- 15 percent of American students speak a foreign language.
- 20 percent of American students live in poverty.
- 15 percent of students have a physical or mental handicap.
- One in four students who leaves middle school in 8th grade fails to graduate. The middle school represents the last chance for schooling for many students.
- One in four American families moves each year.
- Along with fewer children in the average American family, there are fewer adults as well.
- The largest number of adults in the history of the United States held second jobs in the period between 1980 and 1988.

Mental Health of Youth Is a Major Concern in the United States

- National mental health sources show that the second leading cause of death among teenagers, after accidents, is suicide. Each year 6,000 teenagers use a gun, pills, or some other means to kill themselves. Every 90 minutes a teen commits suicide. Every day 1,000 more will attempt it. Teen suicides jumped 256 percent from 1900 to 1983 and tripled between 1976 and 1986.
- Apathy and rejection reflected in our adolescent and postadolescent society are the major contributing factors to the increase in suicides and attempted suicides in the United States. Insecurity in family life is often given as a cause of teenage suicide.
- School stress is Germany and Japan is the reason most given for teenage suicides in those countries.
- Childhood burnout has become a problem for increasing numbers of middle grades students. Students pushed to read early, participate in social events before they are ready and pressured by parents to perform in sports and music at early ages often seek to regain lost childhoods during the teen years by exhibiting childlike behaviors.

The Physical Health of American Youth Is Still Not Good

- Although there has been a massive governmental investment in health care service, about 20 percent of American youth between the ages of 7 and 11 have serious health problems. Many children do not receive proper health care.
- The puberty growth spurt requires an increase in quality food. The diet of teenagers is poor. Surveys show one-half of all middle and high school students don't eat school lunches.
- Gym and health classes for pre-and early adolescents have declined in the past five years. The average adolescent spends six hours daily sitting in front of a television set.
- The average age of beginning smokers dropped from 14 to 10 in the last decade. Sixth graders need help to resist pressure to smoke. Studies show that special programs where high school students learn to say no to smoking reduce the number of smokers.

APPENDIX D

Alcoholism Among Teenagers and Pre-Teens Is Increasing at Alarming Rates

- Alcoholism among teenagers increased 800 percent in the last decade. It is estimated that one of ten students will be an alcoholic by the age of 18.

- Children of alcoholics have a 25-30 percent greater chance of becoming alcoholics themselves. This means 7-14 million children may develop alcoholism if the commonly estimated figure of 10 million adult alcoholics is used.

- By the end of high school one in ten students will suffer a serious drinking problem.

More Youth Are Sexually Active at Earlier Ages

- In 1985 11 million teenagers became pregnant. The percentage rate of those under the age of 15 is beginning to exceed that of late teens. If present trends continue, 30 percent of today's girls will be pregnant by the age of 20.

- 82 percent of teen mothers were the children of teen mothers.

- The rate of child abuse among teenage mothers is especially high due primarily to the immaturity of the mothers.

- Teenage childbearers cost the nation $16.6 billion in 1986.

- Nine years of age is legally considered to be the beginning of childbearing age in most states. Girls' ages of menarche range from 9.1 to 17.7 years. Twenty-five percent of babies born with birth defects are born to adolescent mothers.

- Two-thirds of teenage marriages end in divorce within five years.

- The most frequent reason girls quit school is pregnancy.

Juvenile Delinquency Is a Major Problem in Our Society

- 15,000 murders were committed by teenage boys in 1985.

- Although juveniles (7-18) make up only 20 percent of the population, they account for 43 percent of all serious crimes (murder, rape, robbery). Youth crime is increasing by more than 10 percent a year.

- The peak age for committing violent crime is 14.

- Law education has been mandated for pre- and early adolescents in a number of states.

- Psychologists regard the lack of a stable home as the biggest contributor to delinquency.

- Polls reveal that parents blame themselves for children getting into trouble and not achieving in school but still expect the school to help students overcome problems.

*Sources of Information About American Youth

U.S. Department of Education
National Center For Educational Statistics
National Center For Health Statistics
Department of Agriculture's Food and Nutrition Services
National Institute on Mental Health
National Institute on Drug Abuse
National Institute on Alcohol Abuse and Alcoholism
Census Bureau
National Clearing House for Mental Health Information
National Institute for Child Health and Development
Annual Summary for The United States: Births, Marriages
Divorces, and Deaths, National Center for Health Services
American Association for Physical Education and Recreation

Portrait of a Thirteen Year Old

6 feet 2 inches in height	or	4 feet 7 inches
So awkward that she trips going up the stairs	or	Olympic gold medal winner with a perfect 10.0 in parallel bar competition
Alcoholic, drug addict	or	Sunday school leader, Little Leaguer
Wears mouth braces	or	Competes in Miss Teenage America
Turned off and looking forward to quitting school	or	Curious and enthusiastic learner
Unable to read the comic page	or	Reads the *Wall Street Journal*
Has trouble with whole numbers	or	Can solve geometry problems
A regular in juvenile court	or	An Eagle Scout
Already a mother of two	or	Still plays with dolls

*From Jon Wiles and Joseph Bondi, *The Essential Middle School*, 1986a.

What is a Middle Schooler?

What is a middle schooler?
I was asked one day.
I knew what he was,
But what should I say?

He is noise and confusion.
He is silence that is deep.
He is sunshine and laughter,
Or a cloud that will weep.

He is swift as an arrow.
He is a waster of time.
He wants to be rich,
But cannot save a dime.

He is rude and nasty.
He is polite as can be.
He wants parental guidance,
But fights to be free.

He is aggressive and bossy.
He is timid and shy.
He knows all the answers,
But still will ask "why."

He is awkward and clumsy.
He is graceful and poised.
He is ever changing,
But do not be annoyed.

What is a middle schooler?
I was asked one day.
He is the future unfolding,
So do not stand in his way.

(By an anonymous eighth grade middle school student)

*From Jon Wiles and Joseph Bondi, *The Essential Middle School*, 1986a.